CONTENTS

WH  J YOU

GO TO COURT

Straightforward Publishing
www.straightforwardco.co.uk

Straightforward Publishing

© Straightforward Publishing 2014

ISBN 9781847164452

Printed and bound by Grosvenor Group London

Cover design by Bookworks Islington

stem is complex and daunting and
urt to either resolve disputes or to
ed, will use a solicitor or barrister.
come cheaply. This fact, above all,
ision whether or not to go to court.

ticularly at the time of writing, is
all kinds has been reduced, both
r defendant and also to the legal
that more and more people are
ute of do-it-yourself representation.
litigants-in-person. More and more
self representation and judges will
is book attempts to throw light on
by adopting a specific approach
esses involved.

outline of how the system works
various courts. The Supreme Court
which took effect from October 1st
ole of solicitors and barristers is
and also the book points to other
ilable. Chapter three outlines the
ution to problems before they get to
en long and costly battle. Chapters
esses within the various courts and
which should help the litigant in
rocesses involved.

Overall, this brief but invaluable guide to
own court case, presented through buildi
actual presentation of a case, should prove a
to representing yourself in court.

Introduction

Without doubt, the legal system is complex and daunting and most people who go to court to either resolve disputes or to defend themselves when sued, will use a solicitor or barrister. Such professionals do not come cheaply. This fact, above all, can influence a person's decision whether or not to go to court.

Another consideration, particularly at the time of writing, is the fact that legal aid of all kinds has been reduced, both directly to the claimant or defendant and also to the legal profession with the result that more and more people are choosing to go down the route of do-it-yourself representation. These people are known as litigants-in-person. More and more courts are sympathetic to self representation and judges will often help the litigant. This book attempts to throw light on the whole legal process by adopting a specific approach towards explaining the processes involved.

Chapter one deals with an outline of how the system works and who is who within the various courts. The Supreme Court of the United Kingdom, which took effect from October 1st 2009, is detailed. The role of solicitors and barristers is discussed in chapter two and also the book points to other sources of legal help available. Chapter three outlines the importance of finding a solution to problems before they get to court, as this avoids an often long and costly battle. Chapters four to six outline the processes within the various courts and puts forward case studies which should help the litigant in person gain an idea of the processes involved.

Overall, this brief but invaluable guide to conducting your own court case, presented through building blocks to the actual presentation of a case, should prove an indispensable aid to representing yourself in court.

Ch.1

HOW THE LEGAL SYSTEM WORKS.

HM Courts and Tribunals Services is an arm of the Ministry of Justice. The agency is responsible for the administration of criminal, civil and family courts and tribunals in England and Wales. and non-devolved tribunals in Scotland and Northern Ireland. For more information on HM Courts and Tribunal Service, go to www.justice.gov.uk.

Before deciding to embark upon legal action, whether you are doing so without the aid of a solicitor, or with a solicitor, it is essential to understand the workings of the British legal system. Only then can you begin to conduct a case or to understand how to get the most out of the system.

Legal terms explained

There is a detailed glossary of terms at the back of this book which deals with commonly used legal jargon. However, it is useful to highlight the most common terms right at the outset, as they will be used frequently throughout the book:

Claimant – when legal proceedings are brought, the person or persons, or organisation, bringing the case is called the claimant.

Defendant – The individual or organisation being sued, and therefore defending, is called the defendant.

Solicitor – a solicitor is the lawyer you will (or might) see for legal advice relating to your case. This person will have undertaken many years of study and passed all the necessary legal examinations. We will be discussing solicitors in more depth a little later.

Barrister – A Barrister is a lawyer who is a specialist in what is known as advocacy, i.e. speaking in court. A Barrister will have been called to the bar by one of the Inns of Court and passed the barristers professional examinations. A solicitor will instruct a barrister to represent you in court proceedings. However, barristers will not normally be the persons giving individuals legal advice in the first instance. The legal profession is, basically, split into two, barristers and solicitors, both of whom are lawyers.

Writ – A judicial writ is issued to bring legal proceedings. Civil cases are started in the courts by issuing and serving a writ. This document is completed either by an individual bringing the case or by a solicitor on behalf of the individual. It is issued by the court.

Litigant in person – a litigant is someone who is bringing legal proceedings or suing. A litigant-in-person is someone who chooses to represent themselves in court, without a lawyer.

Damages – Civil claims in the courts are for damages, which is money claimed from the defendant to compensate the claimant for loss arising from the action of default of the defendant. An example might be the sale of a good that has caused injury to a person and it is alleged that the good was faulty at the time of purchase.

Using the legal system to resolve disputes

If you are contemplating any form of legal action, with or without solicitors, it is necessary to have a basic idea of how the system works. The more that you understand the processes underlying the legal system, the more effective you will be, both as a citizen and as a potential litigant.

The structure of the court system

The court system in the United Kingdom deals, in the main, with civil and criminal cases. They are heard in either the county court (civil cases) and the Magistrates and Crown Courts (criminal cases)

Civil cases are those that typically involve breaches of contract, personal injury claims, divorce cases, bankruptcy hearings, debt problems, some employment cases, landlord and tenant disputes and other consumer disputes, such as faulty goods. These are the cases that are most often dealt with by the individual acting as litigant in person.

Criminal cases are those such as offences against the person, theft, damage to property, murder and fraud. These cases, if of a non-serious nature, are heard in the magistrate's courts. If of a serious nature, then they will be heard in the Crown Court and tried by jury. Although individuals do represent themselves in the Crown Court it is more usual to use a solicitor in these cases.

Criminal cases

The more serious criminal cases are tried on the basis of a document called the *indictment.* The defendant is indicted on criminal charges specified in the indictment by the prosecutor. In most cases, the prosecution is on behalf of the Crown (State) and is handled by an official agency called the Crown Prosecution Service, which takes the case over from the police who have already investigated most of the evidence. The first stage will be to decide whether there is a case to answer. This process, called committal, will be dealt with by a magistrate on the basis of evidence disclosed in papers provided by the prosecutor. If the case proceeds, it is heard in the Crown Court. There are about 70 Branches of the Crown Court in the United Kingdom. Addresses can be obtained from the Court service website at HM Courts and Tribunals Service: www.justice.gov.uk. The trial is before a judge and jury. The judge presides over the trial and considers legal issues. The jury will decide on the facts (who is telling the truth) and applies the law to those facts. In criminal cases, the prosecution has to prove, beyond reasonable doubt, that the defendant is guilty. The defendant does not have to prove innocence. However, it is the jury who will observe the prosecutor and defending lawyer and decide the case.

In less serious criminal cases (which comprise over 90% of criminal cases) the case is sent for summary and trial in one of over 400 *magistrates* courts, addresses again from the court service website. A summary trial means that there is no committal or jury. The case is decided by a bench of magistrates. In most cases there are three magistrates who are lay (unqualified) persons but are from the local community. However, there are now an increasing number of 'stipendiary' magistrates, paid magistrates who are qualified lawyers.

Those defendants in criminal cases who are dissatisfied with verdicts may be able to appeal, as follows:

- from the Magistrates courts there is an appeal to the Crown Court on matters of fact or law.
- From the Crown Court, it might be possible to appeal to the Criminal Division of the court of Appeal on matters of fact or law.
- Certain legal disputes arising in the Magistrates court or the Crown Court can be taken before the divisional court of the High Court.
- Matters of important legal dispute arising in the Crown Court can be taken to the Supreme Court (which replaced the House of Lords from October 2009).

Civil cases

The majority of people who buy this book will be taking civil action of one form or another. Increasingly, people are becoming litigants-in-person as this enables people to access the courts and obtain justice without incurring high costs. The only real costs are the court fees (which have increased substantially in 2014) and other incidental costs such as taking time off work and so on.

The county court

The county court deals with civil cases, which are dealt with by a judge, or a district judge. A case can be started in any county court but can be transferred back to the defendant's local court.

All cases arising from regulated credit agreements must be started in the county court, whatever their value.

County courts deal with a wide range of cases ranging from bankruptcy and family matters to landlord and tenant disputes. The most common cases are:

- Consumer disputes, for example faulty goods or services
- Personal injury claims, caused by negligence, for example traffic accidents, accidents caused by faulty pavements and roads, potholes etc
- Debt problems, for example someone seeking payment
- Some undefended divorce cases and some domestic violence cases
- Race and sex discrimination cases
- Employment problems, usually involving pay.

Small claims in the county court

A case in the county court, if it is defended, is dealt with in one of three ways. These ways are called 'tracks' The court will, when considering a case, decide which procedure to apply and allocate the case to one of the following tracks:

- The small claims track

- The fast track
- The multi-track

The small claims track is the most commonly used and is the track for claims of £10,000 or less. Overall, the procedure in the small claims track is simpler than the other tracks and costs are not usually paid by the losing party.

Following a brief summary of the other courts in the United Kingdom, we will be looking in more detail, in chapter 4, at how to commence and process a small claim. In the main, readers of this book will be concerned with the small claims track and it is therefore necessary to outline that process in depth. We will also be looking, in chapter 2, at the legal help scheme. This scheme enables those with a low income to get free legal advice from a solicitor and assistance with preparing a case.

The magistrates' court

As we have seen, magistrate's courts deal with criminal cases in the first instance and also deal with some civil cases. The cases are heard by Justices of the Peace or by District Judges (magistrates courts). All cases heard in a magistrate's court are from within their own area.

Criminal offences in the magistrate's court

Magistrate's courts deal with criminal offences where the defendant is not entitled to a trial by jury. These are known as 'summary offences' and involve a maximum penalty of six months imprisonment and/or a fine up to £5000. Magistrates also deal with offences where the defendant can choose trial by jury. If this is the case, the case is passed up to the Crown Court.

The youth court

The youth court deals with young people who have committed criminal offences, and who are aged between 10-17. The youth court is a part of the magistrate's court and up to three specially trained magistrates hear the case.

If a young person is charged with a very serious offence, which in the case of an adult is punishable by 14 years imprisonment or more, the youth court can commit him/her for trial at the Crown Court.

Civil cases in the magistrates' court

As we have seen, the vast majority of civil cases are dealt with in the county courts. However, the magistrate's court can deal with a limited number of cases, as follows:

- Some civil debts, e.g. arrears of income tax, national insurance contributions, council tax and Value added Tax arrears
- Licences, for example, licences for clubs and pubs
- Some matrimonial problems, e.g. maintenance payments and removing a spouse from the matrimonial home
- Welfare of children, e.g. local authority care orders or supervision orders, adoption proceedings and residence orders

The Crown Court

The more serious criminal cases are tried in the Crown Court. The following are dealt with:

- Serious criminal offences to be heard by judge and jury
- Appeals from the magistrates court-which are dealt with by a judge and at least two magistrates
- Someone convicted in the magistrates court may be referred to the Crown Court for sentencing.

The High Court

The High Court will hear appeals in criminal cases and will also deal with certain civil cases. The High Court also has the legal power to review the actions or activities of individuals and organisations to make sure that they are both operating within the law and also are acting justly. The High Court consists of three divisions, as follows:

The Family Division

The Family Division of the High Court will deal with more complex defended divorce cases, wardship, adoption, domestic violence and other cases. It will also deal with appeals from the magistrates and county courts in matrimonial cases.

The Queens Bench Division

The Queens Bench Division of the High Court will deal with larger claims for compensation, and also more complex cases for compensation. A limited number of appeals from county and magistrates courts are also dealt with. The Queens Bench Division can also review the actions of individuals or organisations and hear libel and slander cases.

The Chancery Division

The Chancery Division deals with trusts, contested wills, winding up companies, bankruptcy, mortgages, charities, and contested revenue such as income tax.

The Court of Appeal

The Court of Appeal deals with civil and criminal appeals. Civil appeals from the high and county courts are heard, as well as from the Employment Appeals Tribunal and the Lands Tribunal. Criminal Appeals include appeals against convictions in the Crown Courts, and points of law referred by the Attorney General following acquittal in the Crown Court or where a sentence imposed is seen as too lenient.

The Supreme Court of the United Kingdom

A new addition to the legal structure of the United Kingdom, the Supreme Court of the United Kingdom was established by the Constitutional Reform Act of 2005. The Court started work on October 1st 2009. It has taken over the judicial functions of the House of Lords, which were exercised by the Lords of Appeal in Ordinary Law (Law Lords), the 12 professional judges appointed as members of the House of Lords to carry out its judicial business. It will also assume some functions of the Judicial Committee of the Privy Council.

The court is the Supreme Court (court of last resort, highest appellate court) in all matters under English law, Welsh law (to the extent that the National Assembly for Wales makes laws for Wales that differ from those in England) and Northern Irish law. It will not have authority over criminal cases in Scotland, where the High Court of Justiciary will remain the supreme criminal court. However, it will hear appeals from the civil court of session, just as the House of Lords did before.

Reasons for creation

The main argument in favour of establishing the court was that the House of Lords role as a legislature and judiciary should be separated.

The Court of First Instance

The Court of First Instance is based in Luxembourg. A case can be taken to this court if European Community law has not been implemented properly by a national government or there is confusion over its interpretation or it has been ignored. A case which is lost in the Court of First Instance may be taken to appeal to the European Court of Justice.

The European Court of Justice of the European Communities

The European Court of Justice advises on interpretation of European Community law and takes action against infringements. It examines whether the actions of those members of the European Community are valid and clarifies European Community law by making preliminary rulings. It also hears appeals against decisions made by the Court of First Instance.

The European Court of Human Rights

The European Court of Human Rights deals with cases in which a person thinks that their human rights have been contravened and for which there is no legal remedy within the national legal system.

Ch. 2

LEGAL HELP

For those contemplating taking legal action, there are a number of options. The first option is usually to visit a solicitor to gain legal help and to launch your case. However, it is a fact that many people are put off going to see a solicitor because of the costs involved. In many cases, unfortunately, this results in people being denied justice.

This book is designed to ensure that those who wish to pursue their own case without the help of a solicitor can do so. Nevertheless, it is very useful indeed to understand what it is exactly that solicitors and barristers do and what their role is within the legal system and to also understand what other forms of legal help are available.

As we have seen, the costs of launching a civil case in the county court are minimal and the process is relatively straightforward. Chapter 4 deals with this process in depth. However, many people would still rather work with the help and guidance of a solicitor. This chapter outlines the work of solicitors, the other forms of legal advice available and also outlines the legal help scheme for those on low income.

Solicitors
Solicitors are trained to deal with a large range of legal problems. Large firms tend to be formed as partnerships and will have specialist solicitors working in defined areas, such as

crime, family, landlord and tenant and so on. Solicitors are heavily regulated by The Law Society and must have no personal interest in the matter in dispute. Solicitors must take out compulsory indemnity insurance to indemnify them against negligence and the profession also runs a 'compensation' fund to compensate those who have suffered loss at the hands of unscrupulous solicitors.

Solicitors do not come cheap and will charge by the hour, charges being anything up to £90 per hour. There are often fixed fees for matters such as conveyancing.

For advice which they consider they may need a second opinion, solicitors will usually seek 'counsels advice' which is given by a barrister. A Barrister is a specialist in advocacy, operating from 'chambers' and costing anything up to £300 per hour. Often, high profile cases, such as tax evasion and libel and slander, will be conducted by barristers.

Anyone considering launching legal action will need to consider whether or not they wish to use a solicitor. For simple small claims, it is not necessary to use a solicitor as the process is designed to assist the layperson. However, the following instances may demand that you use a solicitor:

- Moving house
- Getting divorced (depending on the complexity of the divorce-many straightforward divorced are carried out in person)
- Getting arrested

- Other complex legal matters, such as negligence and nuisance compensation claims

Never use a solicitor without first obtaining an estimate of their likely charges in the matter. Some solicitors will attempt to be vague over such matters but it is highly desirable for you to be assertive on the matters of cost estimates. Ensure that the estimate is in writing and is broken down and clear. Most solicitors now issue a 'client engagement' letter to their clients as recommended by the Law Society.

Solicitor's charges will principally be based on the amount of time spent on the case, as solicitors usually charge by the hour. The longer it takes, the more it will cost you. If the matter is complex, a solicitor will usually look at the case and decide how much they will do and how much a junior will cover, in order to minimise the costs. The notion 'the cheapest is best' is not always correct or advisable when dealing with solicitors, as the quality of advice and degree of organisation will vary according to the solicitors used. Usually, larger practices are better able to offer specialist advice and are also better organised and easier to get access to.

Choosing the right firm

The best way to choose a solicitor is by recommendation, for example one that a friend has used. It will be necessary to ensure that the firm that is recommended has the right experience to represent you adequately.

In some areas, all solicitors will generally have specialism, such as property conveyancing. However, for obtaining compensation for personal injury, or an employment law dispute then you will need to ensure that a firm of solicitors has this expertise.

Using a solicitor

Solicitors are, generally, very thorough and meticulous. They have to be, given the professional standards and codes that they have to deal with and also because of the need to obtain all the facts. It is important that, in the first instance, you give the solicitor as much clear information as possible. Further ongoing contact by telephone is charged for. Most solicitors will monitor calls carefully and enter these in a log or journal. Time is money, so therefore you should ensure:

- All information is passed on at the beginning
- Do not contact the solicitor too often. Ask for regular progress reports to be sent to you
- Respond to requests for information from the solicitor straight away
- Require an initial estimate and notification when costs reach the level of the estimate

Aim for a friendly, professional and open working relationship with a solicitor as you are both striving towards the same goal, that is to win your case.

Finally, if you search on line then you can access a wide range of solicitors and gain an indication of their specialist areas. A word of caution: you should always be wary of those solicitors who advertise on television. Many will say 'no win no fee'. Although this sounds attractive, the fees if you do win can be very high indeed. If you do intend to use such a firm make sure that you understand the charges at the outset.

In some cases, you may be dissatisfied with a solicitor and will wish to complain or even sue. If this is the case then contact the Solicitors Regulation Authority or the Legal Ombudsman (addresses at the back of this book) both of which can be contacted through the Law Society.

Other sources of legal advice

There is no legal requirement to use a solicitor. People do so when they feel that they need advice in the first instance or feel that their case may be too complex. However, there are law centres operating in each local authority area, often offering free advice and specialising in family and community matters, such as health and housing. Citizens Advice Bureau also offer advice and can be found in each area.

In addition, the CAB has on line advice which can be accessed through their web site. This is very useful and has written advice on a wide range of areas.

Some bodies, such as the consumer association, also offer advice, again either by phone or on line, about a range of issues affecting the consumer. In addition, if you are a member of a trade union you may be able to get free legal advice from this source, Some banks offer free legal advice and it is worthwhile giving your local branch a ring.

Financial help

The landscape of legal aid funding has changed considerably since the Conservative Government took power in 2010. The whole are of legal funding, as with all other areas of public expenditure came under intense scrutiny. The bottom line is that financial help for those needing legal aid has been reduced or in some cases eliminated.

Many people will require financial assistance of one sort or another when either taking or defending a legal action. Lack of knowledge and difficulty in meeting costs are the two main reasons for needing assistance.

To oversee the public funding of legal services the Legal Services Commission was created. The Legal Services Commission has now been replaced by the Legal Aid Agency from April 2013.

The Legal Aid Agency

The Legal Aid Agency provides both civil and criminal legal aid and advice in England and Wales.

The Legal Aid Agency is an executive agency of the Ministry of Justice. It came into existence on 1 April 2013 following the abolition of the Legal Services Commission as a result of the Legal Aid, Sentencing and Punishment of Offenders (LASPO) Act 2012.

Financial help
Legal aid for civil cases (non-criminal)

If you need help with paying for legal advice, you may be able to get legal aid. You will have to meet the financial conditions for getting legal aid. In some cases, legal aid is free. In other cases, you may have to pay towards the cost.

Civil legal aid helps you pay for legal advice, mediation or representation in court with problems such as housing, debt and family.

The different types of civil legal aid

There are different types of legal aid which you can get which are:

- Legal Help – advice on your rights and options and help with negotiating
- Help at Court – someone speaks on your behalf at court, but does not formally represent you
- Family Mediation – helps you to come to an agreement in a family dispute after your relationship has broken down without going to court. It can help to resolve problems involving children, money and the family home
- Family Help – help or representation in family disputes like drawing up a legal agreement

- Legal Representation – representation at court by a solicitor or barrister
- Controlled Legal Representation – representation at mental health tribunal proceedings or before the First-tier Tribunal in asylum or immigration cases.

Who can provide legal aid services

Legal aid services can be provided only by organisations which have a contract with the Legal Aid Agency (LAA). These include solicitors in private practice, law centres and some Citizens Advice Bureaux.

What cases can you get civil legal aid for?

You can only get civil legal aid for the following types of cases:

Welfare Benefits

- appeals to the Upper Tribunal, Court of Appeal or Supreme Court.

Council tax reduction schemes

- appeals to the High Court, Court of Appeal or Supreme Court.

Debt

- court action by your mortgage lender because of mortgage arrears.
- court action by a creditor to force you to sell your home
- a creditor is making you bankrupt.

Housing

- court action to evict you from your home because of rent arrears

- eviction from your home
- you are homeless and need help from the council with being re-housed
- your rented home is in serious disrepair
- you are being harassed and need a court order to protect you
- your landlord or the council is taking you to court to get an anti-social behaviour order or anti-social behaviour injunction against you.

Discrimination

- you have been discriminated against and this is against the law. The law protects you from being discriminated against by employers, education, housing and service providers, public bodies such as the Council and associations like sports clubs.

Education (Special Educational Needs)

- appeals against Special Educational Needs assessments by the council

Immigration and asylum

- asylum applications
- you have been detained
- you are applying to settle in the UK (known as indefinite leave to remain) because your relationship has broken down because of domestic violence
- you are an EC citizen and are applying to stay in the UK because your relationship has broken down because of domestic violence

- you are applying to stay in the UK because you are a victim of trafficking
- proceedings before the Special Immigration Appeals Commission
- you have received a Terrorism Prevention and Investigation Measure notice
- applications for asylum support, but only if you have applied for housing and financial support.

Family, children and domestic abuse

You can't get legal aid for most private family law cases such as divorce, or disputes about children and finances unless you're a victim of domestic violence or abuse. Domestic violence or abuse covers psychological, physical, sexual, financial or emotional abuse.

You can get legal aid:

- if you're a victim of domestic violence or are at risk of being a victim of abuse, need advice on your rights to stay in your home and need an order to protect you
- if you're a victim of domestic violence are at risk of being a victim of abuse and need advice on family matters such as divorce, financial disputes or disputes about children
- if you need to protect a child who is at risk of abuse - for example, you need to apply to court to prevent someone who has abused a child from having contact with them
- for family mediation
- for family court proceedings if you are a child

- if you need protection from being forced into marriage or because you have been forced into marriage
- if the local authority is taking court proceedings to take your child into care
- to stop children being removed from the UK or to get them returned if they have been unlawfully removed
- to enforce European Union and international agreements about children and maintenance.

There are very strict rules about the proof that you have to show to qualify for legal aid in these cases.

Mental Health

- advice if someone has been detained or 'sectioned'
- applications to Mental Health Tribunals
- Court of Protection work
- appeals against DOLS (Deprivation of Liberty Safeguards).

Community Care

- for community care cases. Community care services are arranged by the council for people with care needs such as home help.

You can also get legal aid for:

- a court order to protect you from harassment
- an appeal against a decision stopping you from working with children and vulnerable adults
- advice and help on Disabled Facilities Grants
- civil claims relating to allegations of abuse and sexual assault

- confiscation proceedings
- an injunction for gang-related violence
- an inquest into the death of a member of your family
- an injunction to stop a nuisance caused by environmental pollution
- cross-border disputes.

You can't get legal aid for the following types of cases:

- consumer and other contractual disputes
- most immigration cases
- Criminal Injuries Compensation Authority cases
- private family law, for example, divorce, dissolution of civil partnership, property, finance and children matters (other than cases where there is evidence of domestic violence or child abuse)
- personal injury or death
- tort and other general claims
- conveyancing
- advice on will-making
- matters of trust law
- company or partnership law
- business law
- legal advice in relation to a change of name
- defamation or malicious falsehood.

Financial conditions for getting civil legal aid

Your income and capital must be within certain limits to get civil legal aid.

Legal aid if you're getting benefits

If you or your partner receive a passporting benefit, your income will not be looked at to see if you qualify for legal aid. However, your capital will be looked at.

The passporting benefits are:

- Income Support
- income-related Employment and Support Allowance
- income-based Jobseeker's Allowance
- guarantee credit part of Pension Credit
- Universal Credit.

You will get legal aid for an asylum problem if you receive government asylum support.

Legal aid if you have income (figures at 2014)

If your gross monthly income is over £2,657 you won't get legal aid. 'Gross income' means before tax and national insurance are taken off and it excludes certain social security benefits. If you have more than four children, this limit goes up by £222 for the fifth and each additional child. You have to include your partner's income unless your partner is the person who you are in dispute with.

If your gross monthly income is £2,657 or less, your solicitor or adviser will then check what your disposable income is. 'Disposable income' is the amount of income you have left after deductions have been made for national insurance, tax, maintenance, housing costs and certain other expenses. Also, if you have a partner living with you or if you have dependent children or other dependents, a certain amount of your income won't be taken into account. If your partner is earning, their income will be taken into account, unless your partner is the person who you are in dispute with.

To qualify for legal aid, your disposable monthly income can't be more than £733.

If you are within this limit, you don't have to pay anything towards Legal Help. But if your monthly disposable income is over £315, you will have to pay a monthly contribution if you're getting Legal Representation. The amount of the contribution depends on your income.

Legal aid if you have capital

If you have disposable capital (savings) of over £8,000, you won't get legal aid. Disposable capital includes:

- money in the bank
- valuable items
- the value of your home (if you own it). This depends on how much the property is worth and how much your mortgage is.

You have to include your partner's capital unless your partner is the person who you are in dispute with.

If you are getting Legal Representation and your disposable capital is under £3,000, you won't have to pay a contribution towards the costs of your case.

If you have more than £3,000 of disposable capital, you will have to pay a contribution towards the costs of your case. This contribution has to be paid straight away and it will be all of the capital you have over £3,000 up to the total cost of the legal advice.

If you own a home

If you own a home, it will be considered as capital. However, not all the value of your home will be taken into account. You can deduct your mortgage or any charges on your home, up to a maximum of £100,000. This is called mortgage disregard. You can also deduct 3% of the market value of your home (the amount for which it could be sold for on the open market) for sales costs.

Example

The market value of your home is £150,000.
Your mortgage is £90,000.
3 % for sale costs = £4,500.
The capital that's taken into account is £55,500 (£150,000 - £4,500 - £90,000).
If you jointly owned the property, and you owned an equal half, your capital would be £27,500 (half of £55,500).

If you're over 60

If you are over 60, some of your capital can be disregarded in addition to any mortgage disregard. How much of your capital is disregarded depends on how much spare income you have each month. For example, if your spare income is between £0-£25, your disregarded capital is £100,000. If your spare income is between £226-£315 your disregarded capital is £10,000. If your spare income is over £315, none of your capital will be disregarded – although the mortgage disregard may still apply.

Solicitor's costs at the end of your case

If you have had legal aid and the result of your case is that you kept or gained money or property, you will probably have to pay back some or all of the costs of your case. This is called the statutory charge.

At the end of your case, any money you are awarded is normally paid to your solicitor. The legal aid agency will take what has been spent on your solicitor out of the award and you will get what's left.

In some cases, payment of the statutory charge can be postponed if:

- the property you won in the case is your home or the home of your dependants
- the money you won in the case is to be used to buy a home for yourself or your dependants.

Make sure your solicitor or adviser gives you full details about the effects of the statutory charge before you decide to go ahead with your case.

How to apply for civil legal aid

If you're not sure whether you can get legal aid, you can use the 'Can you get legal aid?' tool on the GOV.UK website. Go to www.gov.uk.

The Civil Legal Advice helpline on 0845 345 4345 can also advise you on whether you are eligible for legal aid.

When you apply for legal aid, your legal aid provider should give you the leaflet 'Paying for your civil legal aid'. This can be found at www.justice.gov.uk.

Civil Legal Advice helpline

If you are eligible for civil legal aid, you may be able to get help from the Civil Legal Advice helpline. The Civil Legal Advice helpline gives free, independent and confidential advice on the following matters:

- debt
- housing
- family
- welfare benefits
- discrimination
- education.

The helpline number is: 0845 345 4 345. It is open from 9am to 8.00pm, Monday to Friday and from 9am to 12.30pm on a Saturday. Calls cost no more than 4p a minute from a BT landline. Calls from mobiles are usually more.

If you're worried about the cost of the phone-call, you can ask an adviser to call you back. You can text 'legalaid' and your name to 80010 and an adviser will call you back within 24 hours.

The helpline has a translation service if you would like advice in a language other than English or Welsh.

There is also a minicom service for people who are deaf, hard-of-hearing or speech-impaired and a type-talk service for people with hearing difficulties.

Legal services for deaf people

RAD Legal Services is a legal service providing specialist, independent legal advice in British Sign Language for deaf people. You must have access to a webcam and broadband service and you must be eligible for legal aid. They provide legal advice and representation on the following subjects:

- debt
- housing
- family
- welfare benefits
- discrimination
- education.

You can get further information and help from their website at www.deaflawcentre.org.uk.

Legal aid for criminal cases

Legal aid in criminal cases is organised by the Legal Aid Agency. There are different types of help you might be able to get, depending on your circumstances.

You should get advice from a solicitor who will assess whether you are eligible for legal aid.

Free legal advice at the police station

If you are at the police station, you have the right to free independent legal advice from a duty solicitor. This does not depend on your financial circumstances. Your request will be passed to the Defence Solicitor Call Centre. Alternatively you can choose your own solicitor and won't have to pay for advice if they have a contract with the Legal Aid Agency. The Call Centre will contact your solicitor for you.

If you're under arrest, you have the right to consult a solicitor at any time unless it is a serious case when this right can be postponed. You must be given an information sheet explaining how to get legal help.

Help before you're charged with a criminal offence

You could get help with a criminal case even if you haven't been charged with a criminal offence. For example, a solicitor could give general advice, write letters or get a barrister's opinion. This type of help is called Advice and Assistance.

You will get Advice and Assistance if you get Income Support, income-related Employment and Support Allowance, income-based Jobseeker's Allowance, the guarantee credit part of Pension Credit or Universal Credit. If you get Working Tax Credit, you might get Advice and Assistance depending on your income and personal circumstances.

If you are not getting one of these benefits or Working Tax Credit, you will only get Advice and Assistance if your income and savings are below a certain amount.

You should get advice from a solicitor who will assess whether you are eligible for advice and assistance.

Help with representation at court

There are three ways you could be helped if you need to be represented in court for a criminal offence.

Representation Order

A Representation Order covers representation by a solicitor and, if necessary, by a barrister in criminal cases.

To qualify for a Representation Order in the magistrates' court, you must meet certain financial conditions. You'll automatically meet these conditions if you're under 18. Also you'll automatically meet the conditions if you're getting Income Support, income-related Employment and Support Allowance, income-based Jobseeker's Allowance, the guarantee credit part of Pension Credit or Universal Credit. Otherwise, the financial conditions depend on your gross income and whether you have a partner and/or dependent children. If your gross annual income, which when adjusted to take into account any partner or children, is over £22,325, you will not be eligible for a Representation Order. However, in some cases it may be possible to apply for a review on the grounds of hardship.

If you do meet the financial conditions, you'll usually get help with representation in a criminal case in the magistrates' court, as long as it's in the interests of justice that you are legally represented. This means, for example, if you are likely to go to prison or lose your job if you are convicted.

In the Crown Court, it will automatically be in the interests of justice that you are legally represented. But you might have to contribute towards the cost of your legal representation from your income or capital.

If you have a disposable income above £283.17 per month, you will have to make five contributions from your income. If you are late paying, you will have to make one extra payment.

If you are found guilty and have capital over £30,000, you may be asked to pay a contribution from your capital.

However, you will not be entitled to legal aid representation if your disposable annual income is £37,500 or more and you will have to pay privately for your costs.

If you are found not guilty, your payments will be refunded to you.

To apply for a Representation Order, ask for an application form at the court dealing with your case or speak to your solicitor.

Advocacy Assistance

Advocacy Assistance covers the costs of a solicitor preparing your case and initial representation in certain cases such as:

- prisoners facing disciplinary charges
- prisoners with a life sentence who are referred to the Parole Board
- warrants of further detention.

You don't have to meet any financial conditions to qualify for Advocacy Assistance, except if it's a prison hearing.

Free advice and representation at the magistrates' court

If you didn't get legal advice before your case comes up at the magistrates' court, you can get free legal advice and representation by the court duty solicitor. This does not apply to less serious cases such as minor driving offences but it could cover cases of non-payment of council tax.

You do not have to meet any financial conditions to get free advice and representation at the magistrates' court.

The court staff will tell you how to find the duty solicitor.

Paying court fees if you are getting legal aid

If you wish to start court action, you will need to pay a court fee. You can find further information about court fees on the HM Courts and Tribunal Service website at www.justice.gov.uk. If you're on a low income, you can get help with paying all or some of the court fee. This is called a fee remission.

If you are receiving Legal Representation or Family Help (Higher) you cannot apply for a fee remission as your solicitor will pay your court or tribunal fee for you. If you receive advice under Family Help (Lower) where a consent order is being applied for, your solicitor will also pay your court or tribunal fees for you.

You can apply for a fee remission if you are receiving:

- Legal Help
- Help at Court
- Family Help (Lower) except where a consent order is being applied for.

You can ask the court to tell you how to apply for a fee remission or you can get more information and the form EX 160A which can be used to apply for a fee remission from HM Courts and Tribunals Service at www.justice.gov.uk

Ch. 3

SOLVING DISPUTES BEFORE TAKING LEGAL ACTION

If you are in dispute and feel that you need to revert to using the law, before you do so you should try to solve the dispute amicably. You need to establish the facts of the matter and examine whether or not there actually is a dispute at all or whether the problem could be solved without recourse to the law. You also need to look at the dispute in terms of whether or not realistically you are going to win or whether you will be involved in a long and drawn out expensive battle that you are unlikely to win.

You should ask yourself the following questions before committing a case to court:

- Is your case clear cut or does your opponent have a clear argument?
- What do others think about your case? You need to ask someone who is unbiased.
- What is the value of your claim/ Does it justify the time and expense of going to court?
- What are the likely solicitors (if any at any point) costs?

Payments into court

If you do go to court, it is worth noting that the defendant can pay a sum into court, representing the amount of money for which the defendant would settle. If the case proceeds and the plaintiff wins less than that sum, then the defendant will not have to pay the plaintiffs costs. You should always think carefully about accepting a payment into court and should take legal advice.

Timing of court action

Court actions can, by their very nature, be slow and painstaking. However, the timing depends very much on the nature of the dispute. In cases of emergency where an order is needed to prevent someone from doing something this can be made in a matter of hours. These are known as 'injunctions'. Most disputes, however, often take many months to go through the court procedure. So do not expect a quick victory, as the wheels of justice turn at their own pace.

Damages

Damages is the money which is won in compensation from the defendant. The judge in the dispute will make the order as to damages, which normally consists of a sum of money necessary to place the claimant in the same position as he or she was before the incident occurred. There is an obligation to 'mitigate' loss, which means that the claimant should take reasonable care to reduce the loss as much as possible.

Damages can be reduced where the claimant is at fault, for example where the claimant has added to the injury suffered by his or her own actions at the time and subsequently.

Damages for criminal injury

In cases where a criminal injury has occurred and compensation cannot be obtained from the perpetrator, you may be able to get compensation from the Criminal Injuries Compensation Authority. The CICA gives out compensation amounting to millions of pounds each year. The address of the Authority is found at the rear of this book.

The eligibility requirements of the programme are that the matter must be reported to police as soon as possible after it has occurred. The matter has to be filed to the CICA within two years. Those who can claim are:

- Victims of crime
- Dependants of homicide victims
- Foreign citizens

Procedures

A claimant can obtain an application from CICA, local victim support schemes, Crown Court witness service, local police stations or local citizens advice bureau. The application should be sent to CICA. The authorities initial decision should be made within 12 months, while reviews and hearings can take several months longer. Compensation can be paid as soon as CICA is notified that the claimant accepts the decision.

Benefits and award limits

The maximum award is £500,000.

Compensable costs

- Medical expenses
- Mental Health expenses
- Lost wages for disabled victims
- Lost support for dependants of homicide victims
- Funerals
- Travel
- Rehabilitation for disabled victims
- Pain and suffering
- Bereavement
- Loss of parental services

Emergency awards

Interim payments can be made where a final decision as to the appropriate award is uncertain. For example, where the victim's medical prognosis is unclear.

Funding

The programme is funded by the taxpayer

Appealing against a CICA decision

There is an appeals panel, which will hear appeals against the findings of the CICA. Details can be obtained from the headquarters of CICA.

What to do if you are sued.

In addition to deciding to sue someone, you may find yourself in receipt of a summons or writ through the post. The summons or writ will always provide for a written defence, which has to be filed within a time periods clearly outlined on the document. If you do not file the defence then a judgement will be entered against you automatically.

When receiving a writ or summons the following actions should be taken:

- Check to whom the document is addressed. It may be that it should be for someone else. If this is the case forward it on or return to the sender
- If it is for you read it very carefully indeed. With the summons will be a particulars of claim which will outline what the case is against you
- Note any time limits that you have to adhere to

What form of action you should take will very much depend on the nature of the writ or summons. As we discussed, the case will either be civil or criminal. Most people are aware of the basic criminal offences, such as driving offences etc. A small claim against you could be for a variety of actions, such as breach of contract or negligence.

Most criminal offences require attendance at court. Minor criminal offences require attendance at the magistrate's court. Civil offences will require attendance at County Court if you decide to defend. If you admit a claim then the matter can be settled by post.

In criminal offences, the judge will pass sentence. In civil cases, the judge will enter a judgement and decide on a level of compensation relevant to the action.

If the defendant does not pay the money arising from the judgement, then the following remedies are available:

- Send in the bailiffs to seize goods to the value of the claim.
- Attachment of earnings so that the award is taken directly from the persons salary
- Charging orders over the defendants property
- Garnishee orders that can order money to be taken from a bank account.

Ch. 4

PROCEDURE IN THE CROWN COURT

In Chapter 1, we discussed the nature of the Crown Court. As we saw, the Crown Court deals mainly with criminal cases. The process is heavily procedural and each case follows a set pattern. It is not usual for a defendant or prosecution to present a case without the aid of lawyers. Some people, however, choose to do this and the following outlines a case and how it is conducted using a solicitor. The litigant in person will follow exactly the same procedure.

It is highly advisable to have some idea of court procedures before a do-it-yourself presentation of a case. The procedure, however, will remain the same.

The Jury

A jury consists of 12 people and their job is perhaps one of the most important in the whole Crown Court procedure. A Jury is randomly chosen from the local public, between the ages of 18-70 and their job, in a criminal case, is to listen to all the evidence about the facts of a case. They will often have to make hard decisions concerning who to believe or not, when differing versions of what happened are given by the defence and prosecution. At the end of a trial, the jury retires in private and must decide the guilt or innocence of the person charged. The prosecution must prove the case against the defendant on each charge so that the jury are sure of guilt.

The job of a juror can be complicated and disturbing. Quite often, the charges are quite harrowing and the evidence is not that clear. The juror, or jurors, must fight against their own prejudices and must avoid jumping to conclusions.

The following represents basic advice concerning the procedure relating to jurors.

The Court Service produces a booklet called 'You and Your Jury Service'. Further advice can be obtained from the Court Service website. This outlines the role of the juror in more detail. If a court writes to a juror and informs them that they have been selected for jury service, they will send a letter that is filled in stating that either they are able to carry out jury service or asking for reasons why not. The court will:

- Let a juror know at least four weeks before they are needed
- Send a jury summons which sets out the rules about jury service and tells them if they can be let off serving as a juror
- Send a booklet 'You and Your Jury Service' which explains more about the duty of a juror and also details expenses and allowances that can be claimed.

- An information leaflet will be sent which includes a map, details of public transport and where to park, the times of opening, details of refreshments etc.

When a juror arrives at court they will be shown to a separate sitting room for jurors and shown a video which explains the job of a juror in more detail. They can also talk with a customer service officer in private if they wish.

How a jurors time is used

Some people may not be able to sit as jurors on certain trials because, for example, they are connected with the defendant or the case. The court service always summons more jurors than they need because it is difficult to prepare for all circumstances. Normally, a length of service will be five days. Some jurors are needed for all five days others can be let off early. The court service will:

- Try to use time as a juror efficiently
- Tell a juror every hour when you may be needed in court
- Let them go as soon as possible if they are not needed
- Let them go back to work on days or part days when they are not needed, if an employer agrees with this.
- Give the juror a special number to phone (in larger Crown Courts) to find out if they need to come to court that day

Complaining about Jury Service

If a juror wants to complain about jury service then a member of staff will first try to sort out the problems then and there. If they are still not happy they can refer their complaint to the customer service manager. They can also write to the court manager. They may be able to claim compensation if they have run up costs because of court mistakes.

Inside a Crown Court
Court etiquette

All courts are formal. The whole ethos underpinning the dispensation of justice is underpinned by formality. This is because the events that happen within a courtroom are very serious, can lead to the deprivation of liberty and therefore must be treated with an appropriate gravity.

When attending court:

- Remove all headgear before entering the court. There are exceptions for religious observances.
- Enter and leave the courtroom at an appropriate time so as to cause as little disturbance as possible.
- Keep quiet at all times.
- Sit in the designated areas, which will be pointed out to you by the usher.
- Stand when the judge enters or leaves the court.
- Always ask the usher if you are in any doubt as to what to do.

The following activities are not permitted in court:

- Smoking
- Eating and drinking.
- Reading magazines and newspapers.
- Taking photographs.
- Making tape recordings
- Using a mobile phone.
- Using a personal stereo.
- Taking notes (unless authorised to do so by the usher).
- Bringing an animal into court (with the exception of guide dog for the blind).

The Judge

The judge presides over the trial and tries to ensure clarity and fairness. The judge will decide on legal issues such as whether evidence is admissible (i.e. what the jury is allowed to take into account).

The judge must remain apart from other people in a trial and therefore has a separate entrance and a private office called 'Judges chambers'. If you have decided to represent yourself without the aid of a barrister then it is highly likely that the judge will provide some guidance without prejudicing his or her position.

Barristers

We have already discussed the role of barristers and solicitors in chapter one. Barristers (or counsel) are qualified lawyers who represent the prosecution or the defendant (in criminal cases) or the defendant or claimant (in civil cases). Barristers have special training in courtroom procedure and advocacy (presenting cases in court). They sit in the courtroom facing the judge and are responsible for explaining the case, arguing its merits and, most importantly, presenting the case by calling the evidence upon which the case is decided.

Solicitors

Solicitors are qualified lawyers. They work with their client and the barrister, preparing the case and collecting the evidence. Some solicitors have received special training and are qualified to act as advocates in the Crown Court. Solicitors can present cases in the magistrates and county courts. In a criminal case, the defence solicitor is appointed by the defendant. The lawyers representing the prosecution will usually be employed by the Crown Prosecution Service. Solicitors and their employees who assist counsel in the Crown Court sit behind them. In a civil case, each side chooses its own lawyers.

Clerks

The clerk, sometimes called the associate, looks after all the documents for the trial, and records all the judges decisions and instructions, so that they can be acted upon.

The clerk is responsible for some of the most important formalities: he or she reads out the 'indictments' (telling the defendant what he or she is charged with) ensures that the jury takes a solemn oath to give a true verdict according to the evidence and that the witness takes a solemn oath to tell the truth. At the end of the trial they ask the jury what their verdict is. This is called 'taking the verdict'.

The Usher

The usher looks after the courtroom and the people in it including the judge and jury. The usher will also bring into court the defendants, witnesses and others required by the court.

The Crown Prosecution Service

The Crown Prosecution Service work closely with the police and:

- Prosecute people in England and Wales who have been charged by the police with a criminal offence
- Advise the police on possible prosecutions
- Review prosecutions or possible prosecutions
- Review prosecutions started by the police to ensure the right defendants are prosecuted on the right charges before the appropriate court
- Prepare cases for court
- Prosecute cases at magistrate's courts and instruct counsel to prosecute cases in the Crown Court and higher courts.

- Work with others to improve the effectiveness and efficiency of the criminal justice system

The CPS, although working closely with the police is independent of them.

The Defendant

This is the person who has been accused of a crime and is standing trial for this in the court. In a criminal case sometimes two or more people are accused of committing a crime together.

Witnesses

During the trial the witnesses are brought one by one into the witness box to give evidence, i.e. to tell the court what they can about the facts of a case. First, the witnesses for the prosecution are called. Their evidence must be limited to things that they have seen or heard themselves. Experts may also be called on to give authoritative opinions on subjects such as fingerprints, guns or medical matters.

Next, the witnesses for the defence are called. They may include the defendant and other witnesses, including, for example, 'alibi witnesses' (if the defendant denies being present at the scene and the witness can say where he was) and the defences own experts.

If there is no dispute between the prosecution and the defence over the evidence of a witness, the witness is not called and instead the evidence is agreed and read to the jury as 'agreed evidence'.

Where a witness is vulnerable or worried about giving evidence he or she may be supported through the experience by a member of the witness support team. They will look after the witness outside the court and remain in court when the witness is giving evidence.

More details about the witness Support Team can be obtained from the court office.

The press

The press or other representatives of the media usually sit at the front of the public seating area (or in other reserved seats) to report what happens in court for the benefit of the public in general. They are entitled to report any part of the court proceedings providing the reports are accurate and fair.

The court may order that they cannot report on proceedings if there is some good legal reason that they should not do so e.g. if children are involved, or matters of law are being discussed in the absence of the jury.

The Public

Any member of the public may sit in the public seating area to see and hear what is happening.

Court Reporter

Many cases are officially recorded as they proceed by a court reporter who is responsible for recording the evidence and the judges summing-up (in criminal cases) and the judgement (in civil cases).

Dock Officer

In the Crown Court the defendant who is accused of a crime is accompanied by a dock officer who is responsible for his/her security.

The above represent the personnel who are key players in the process of a trial.

We will now look at a case study which will help put the whole trial process in context. is a case study outlining the procedures in a Crown Court trial

Case study

Guide to a criminal case

The following constitutes the procedure in a criminal case.

Background to the case.

Peter, 18, has been arrested and charged with four offences-theft (robbing an off-licence of wine and beer) assault (hitting the shopkeeper in the face and breaking his jaw), possessing an offensive weapon (a knife) and damage to property (breaking a window and damaging shop furniture).

Peter told his lawyers that he didn't do any of the above and he has been set up by the shopkeeper, who knows and dislikes him. He said that he had merely gone into the shop to buy wine and beer, had met a friend and absentmindedly taken beer and wine whilst he was talking, and he was told by the shopkeeper that he would not be served. The shopkeeper attacked him and Peter acted in-self defence. He also stated that he did not have a knife. There was a customer in the shop at the time who saw what happened.

Peter is represented by a solicitor who has 'briefed' or 'instructed' a barrister to act as Peters advocate-that is to present his case in court. Peter will have met the solicitor who is preparing his case on a number of occasions. He will probably meet his barrister for the first time before the trial.

The prosecution are also represented by a barrister briefed by the Crown prosecution Service.

Some weeks ago Peter appeared before the magistrates. Then the prosecution solicitor explained the evidence against him. Peter did not have to say what his explanation was. The magistrates said there was enough evidence for Peter to stand trial in the Crown Court before judge and jury.

The judge runs the trial and must ensure it is conducted fairly at all times. The judge has to decide what evidence can be allowed and what cannot. He or she has to advise the jury what the law is and, if Peter is found guilty, the judge will decide what sentence to give. He or she wears judicial robes (a wig and gown) and remains apart from everyone else involved.

As stated, the jury has to listen to all the evidence about the facts. They will often have to decide which witness to believe or not to believe when different versions of what happened are given by different people. They must then decide, in private, whether the defendant is guilty or not. The prosecution must prove the case against the defendant on each charge so that the jury are sure of guilt.

The procedure

Prosecuting: the charge

Everyone who is accused of a crime must know and understand clearly what it is they are said to have done. This must be in writing.

The clerk reads out each charge and asks Peter if he is guilty or not guilty.

The defence

As the charges are read out, Peter says 'not guilty' to each charge. The jury is sworn in. Twelve members of the public, selected at random, are asked to swear that they will give a true verdict 'according to the evidence'. The juror has the choice to swear or affirm, depending on religious belief. If Peter has a good reason he can object to any of the jurors. For example, if one is a friend, or a teacher at his old school he can object.

The prosecution opening speech

The barrister appearing for the prosecution will make a short opening speech to the judge and jury telling them what the case is all about. He has to summarise both what the prosecution say happened and what Peter says happened.

Prosecution evidence

Each witness who saw what happened is called to give evidence. Usually the victim goes first. So in this case, the prosecution calls:

- the shopkeeper
- the other customer in the shop
- the police who were called and who arrested Peter
- the doctor who examined the shopkeeper
- the forensic scientist who found Peters fingerprints on the knife.

Each witness swears to tell the truth or affirms that he or she will do so. The prosecution barrister asks questions of these witnesses first. The questions must not suggest the 'right' answer. These are called 'leading questions'. So for example he cannot ask the shopkeeper 'did you see Peter steal the wine and beer' he must ask 'what did you see Peter do?'

Cross- examination

The barrister representing Peter can test the evidence of each of the prosecution's witnesses by asking any questions which are relevant to the case. It is the best opportunity to show that the witness is unreliable or cannot remember things clearly-or is even dishonest.

When Peters barrister put it to the shopkeeper that he chased Peter and fell down as he reached him, injuring himself, he admitted that he could not be sure whether Peter hit him before he fell or it just felt like that and he was confused.

If the defence disagrees with what a witness has said they must make this clear.

The prosecution

When the policeman who arrested Peter said he found the knife in Peters pocket, Peters barrister has to suggest to him that, as Peter says that he never had a knife, the policeman must have placed it there. Peter's barrister has finished his cross-examination and the defence is asked if they have any further questions. At this point he declines.

The defence opening speech

The defence barrister can make a speech but does not have to and is not allowed to if Peter is the only defence witness on his side. The defence rarely makes a speech at this stage – saving things for later.

The defence evidence

The witnesses on Peter's side now give evidence. Usually the defendant, Peter in this case, goes first.

He does not have to give evidence but if he does not the jury can draw inferences from his failure to do so. The jury may think that he has something to hide, as he was the best-placed person to say what he believed happened.

Cross examination of defence witnesses

In this case, Peter gives evidence, repeating his story originally given to the police. Other witnesses on Peter's side also give evidence. His only real witness in this case was his friend Dave who he had met in the shop and talked to. Dave confirmed that Peter was notoriously absent minded and would not have deliberately stolen the beer and wine but was indeed only putting them into his bag.

This is the prosecution's opportunity to challenge Peter and any other witness on his side. This can be very direct and personal. The way in which Peter gives his evidence and replies to challenging questions can be the key for the jury to make up their minds on the truth of the case.

In this case:

- Peter admitted under questioning that he had an alcohol habit and had treatment for this habit.
- Dave admitted that he knew Peter had bought a knife. He couldn't identify it though as the one the police said that they had found on Peter.
- The other customer maintained that although the shopkeeper was angry and chased after Peter he had not seen Peter hit him.

> *Prosecution closing speech*

The prosecution barrister makes a final speech to the jury explaining how he says the charges are proved.

Defence closing speech

The defence barrister makes a closing speech and explains to the jury why he says that the evidence does not amount to sure proof that Peter did what he is accused of.

Judges summing up

The judge first tells the jury what the law is on each charge and what the prosecution must prove in order to make the jury sure of the case. He then reminds them of the important parts of the evidence from both sides. This must be fair and balanced.

Reaching a verdict

The jury will retire to a separate room. This will be guarded by a 'jury bailiff' who is an usher. The jury must elect a 'foreman' of the jury who will act as an unofficial chair and will announce the verdict in court. Juries must not discuss the case with anyone else, even if they go home overnight.

Juries are expected to reach a unanimous verdict. If they have tried for a long time the judge can agree to accept a majority verdict which must be at least 10-2. If that is not possible the jury is said to disagree and the defendant must go through a retrial. If the same thing happens a second time the custom is that the prosecution is dropped and the defendant is found not guilty.

The verdict

If the jury finds the defendant not guilty then he can leave the court immediately as a free man. He cannot then be tried again for the same offence (although there are currently proposals to change this in certain circumstances).

If he is found guilty the judge must pass sentence. In this case, Peter is found guilty of theft and possessing an offensive weapon, but he is found not guilty of assault.

The judge now has to sentence Peter. He will take everything he knows about the case into account. He will be told if Peter has any previous convictions. He will not sentence Peter until he has received pre-sentence reports from the probation service.

Plea in mitigation

Peter's barrister can explain to the judge why a light sentence is more appropriate than a severe one. He can produce references for him and explain any relevant personal circumstances about work or family life. The judge will also have a pre-sentence report prepared by a probation officer. All of this can be very important in helping a judge to decide between a sentence of custody and some other punishment.

Sentence

In this case Peter has past convictions for stealing and violence. He has been fined and placed on probation. The judge has the following choices:

- Rehabilitation (probation)

- Community punishment (unpaid work on behalf of the community

- Custody in a young offender institution (Peter is under 21 so cannot be sent to prison)

- As Peter's offences include theft, violence and possessing an offensive weapon, and he has a previous conviction he is sentenced to eight months in a young offender institution.

The dock officer who has been escorting peter to the dock will take him down to the courts cells prior to transferring him to an institution.

Refer overleaf for summary of trial process.

Summary of trial process in the Crown Court

1. Prosecution – the charge is read to the defendant.
2. The defendant pleads guilty or not guilty.
3. The prosecution makes the opening speech.
4. The prosecution gives evidence. Witnesses are called.
5. The defendant's barrister cross-examines the prosecution witnesses.
6. The defence barrister makes an opening speech.
7. The defence calls witnesses.
8. The prosecution cross-examines witnesses for the defence.
9. The prosecution makes a closing speech to the jury.
10. The defence makes a closing speech to the jury.
11. The judge sums up the case.
12. The jury retire to reach a verdict.
13. The verdict is announced.
14. The defence barrister can make a plea in mitigation.
15. The judge will pass sentence.

Ch. 5

PROCEDURE IN THE COUNTY COURTS

In chapter one, we briefly discussed the nature of county courts. In this chapter, we will look at county courts in more depth and also the procedure in a civil case, much as we looked at the procedure in a criminal case in the previous chapter. The case study outlined will help to outline the civil case procedure, specifically in relation to personal compensation. In the following chapter, we will look in depth at making a small claim for faulty goods and services.

County Courts
These courts were created by the County Courts Act 1846. They deal with the majority of the civil disputes, acting as local courts dealing with small claims. There are 54 "circuits" or areas in the country, each circuit having one or more judges assigned to it, resulting in about 400 courts in England and Wales

The civil procedure rules
County courts are governed by the Civil Procedure Rules which guide the actions of the county courts and of claimants and defendants.

Circuit judges

Circuit judges were created by the Courts Act 1971 and are appointed from barristers of at least 10 years standing

Registrars

Registrars conduct the administrative work of county courts. They are civil servants and must be solicitors of seven years standing. They have jurisdiction to try cases where the amount is less than £500 pounds

County Court jurisdiction

County courts have a range of responsibilities:

- Hearing cases and tort (negligence) up to £5000 pounds, although there is no limit if both parties agree
- Housing and landlord and tenant disputes-the court will consider cases where the title to land and recovery of possession of land, concerns a net annual value for rating of less than £2000 pounds. The court also decides on matters under the Rent Act 1977, the Landlord and Tenant Act 1954 (Business tenancies), the Housing Act 1985, 1988 and 1996 and the Commonhold and Leasehold Act 2004.
- The County Court will also hear matters where an aggrieved person has a statutory right or legal right of appeal in housing matters
- Considering matters of equity such as trusts, mortgages and dissolution of partnerships where the amount is less than £30,000 pounds

- Hearing petitions for bankruptcy and winding up of companies with a paid up share capital not exceeding £20,000 pounds
- Uncontested hearings under the Matrimonial Causes Act 1967, or Nullity of marriage. If they are contested they will be transferred to the High Court
- Hearing disputes concerning the grant of probate or letters of administration, where the estate of the deceased person is less than £15,000 pounds

The jurisdiction of the County Court is limited to the locality it is in: cases should be commenced in the court in the area where the defendant resides or carries on business or where the cause of the action arises. There are more than three times as many proceedings commenced in the County Court than in all the divisions of the High Court which deals with all other Civil Disputes

Small Claims procedure

The County court hears small claims actions up to £50,000 pounds although if it is a significant amount it is likely to be heard by a Tribunal. We will be discussing small claims in more depth later on in this book.

Tribunals

The enormous growth in the work of the courts in modern times, coupled with the relatively high costs of bringing a court action, has led to an increase of the number of tribunals.

Tribunals deal with disputes in particular areas of the law and attempt to do so in a less formal and speedier manner than would be possible through the ordinary courts

Tribunals are independent and impartial bodies, using the same rules of evidence under oath as the ordinary courts, although the Tribunal members may comprise both legally qualified and lay members. Procedures may be heard in a Tribunal having been referred from a court

Civil cases in the County Court

We have seen in the previous chapter that trials in the Crown, or High, Courts are usually trials by jury and the Crown Prosecution Service is involved.

Cases in the county courts are cases held without jury, with the judge having the final say. This is because the county courts deal with non-criminal matters, small claims, between individuals and organisations. As with the High Court, the procedure is formal and regulated and there is a set process to go through when preparing and presenting a claim. In the county court, the person taking the case to court is called the 'claimant' and the person defending is called the 'defendant'. Neither party has to be represented by a solicitor. Many people who use the county courts chose to present their own cases. As we have seen, although this can be the case in the High court it is not the norm.

In the next chapter there is an outline of the small claims procedure relating to money judgements. In these cases, a solicitor is not usually used. However, in many other cases, a solicitor is used and the following case outlines the procedure where a person is defended.

Case study outlining the county court procedure

Sandra was in the women's toilet at an airport. The airport is controlled by the British Airports Authority. She entered a cubicle and locked the door after her. However, when she tried to get out she found that the door would not open. Sandra panicked, as she realised that her flight was leaving very soon. She decided to clamber over the top of the door, as her cries for help went unheeded. She stood on the door handle, which snapped and she fell backwards, badly spraining her wrist and breaking her ankle.

Sandra decided to claim compensation from the BAA stating that they were negligent and to blame for the faulty lock. In short, they are responsible for her injury and subsequent missed flight and time off work.

On reflection, Sandra has decided to instruct a firm of solicitors to act for her. She knows that she can represent herself in the county court but has decided that the matter might get complicated and that the BAA will pay more attention to a firm of solicitors.

Before the case goes to court, Sandra's solicitors must fill in a claim form and send this to court. The claim form is the form used to start all cases in the county court and sets out Sandra's version of events and states why she is entitled to compensation.

The British Airports Authority disputes the claim and have to present their defence. This sets out their case and states why Sandra should not receive any compensation.

Both sides may obtain evidence – that is statements from witnesses to support their side of the case, which sets out what they say happened.

As Sandra is claiming less than £15,000 compensation and the case should be dealt with quickly, it is heard in the local county court before a district judge. If it involved more than £15,000 or was seen to be more complicated it would be heard either in a county court by a more senior judge or in the High Court by a High Court Judge, but the proceedings would be similar.

As explained, there is no jury in most civil cases – so the judge hears the case on his or her own. The judge will have been involved in the early stages of the case making sure that both sides have their cases ready for trial. Judges now have to 'manage' cases they are going to hear in order to make sure they are dealt with as quickly and efficiently as possible. In court the judge must decide on the basis of the evidence what has actually happened and then has to apply the law to settle who was actually responsible. If the case is proved the judge will decide how much compensation to award to Sandra.

In a civil trial a claimant does not have to make the judge sure that he or she is right. They have to prove the case on a 'balance of probabilities'. This means that their case is more often right than not. The judge will wear judicial robes and a wig and will sit apart from everyone else.

The case

> *Claimant's opening speech*

At the outset of the case, Sandra's solicitor makes a short opening speech to the court which explains what the case is and what evidence will be called to prove it. The solicitor will also summarise what the defendant says the position is.

> *Claimant's evidence*

The claimant – Sandra – is usually called to give evidence first and says what happened.
Other witnesses who help her to prove her claim give evidence. So here, her lawyer calls:

- her friend who had been waiting for her outside. She had eventually gone back into the toilet and heard Sandra in pain in the locked cubicle

- the doctor who examined her and reported on her injuries
- other people who had used the toilet in the recent past and had reported that the lock was sometimes jamming and defective.

An important piece of evidence here, perhaps the most important piece, was the state of the lock-was it faulty or was it a one-off incident, not down to negligence.

This is something an expert can decide and the court has ordered a single expert to examine the state of the lock and report on the problem. This saves arguments between different experts on what should be an uncomplicated technical matter. The expert said that, in this case, the lock was faulty.

Cross examination

This is where the lawyer representing the defendant (the counsel) will test what has been said by the claimant and witnesses. It is an opportunity to show that their memory is shaky or the evidence was exaggerated or made up. The questions can be very direct or personal.

In this case, Sandra accepts that she must have realised that the door handle was probably not going to withstand her weight and could break. Therefore, she knowingly put herself at risk.

Re-examination

This is a chance for Sandra's solicitor to ask further questions to clear up any confusion. However, he cannot ask about new things.

Defendants opening speech

The barrister representing the Airports Authority can make a short speech introducing the evidence he is going to call. However, often the witnesses are called straight away.

Defendant's evidence

The witnesses on the Airport Authority's side now give evidence. In this case, an employee of the BAA gives evidence as to how often the toilets are checked for damage to doors. In addition, he gives evidence concerning any other reports of people being trapped.

The employee explains that if Sandra had called out it would have been heard quite clearly by a number of people and explained that he had heard nothing until Sandra's friend had reported the problem.

The Airport Authority accepted the expert's evidence that at the time he inspected the lock it was faulty and the doctor's evidence about Sandra's injuries.

Cross examination

This is the opportunity for Sandra's solicitors to challenge the defendant's witnesses. The employee of BAA admitted that, as he was concentrating on other things at the time he probably would not have heard the cries for help, unless it was very loud.

In addition, the records did not show that the lock had been inspected or who had carried out the checks. So Sandra's solicitor suggested that there was real doubt about whether there had been an effective recent inspection.

Defendant's closing speech

The Airport Authority's barrister now makes a speech to the court which reviews all the evidence and explains why the BAA says that it wasn't reasonable for them to be held responsible for Sandra's injuries.

He says that the BAA accepts that the lock was faulty but they had carried out all reasonable checks and, at the end of the day, although Sandra was injured, in some respects this was down to her own actions not the BAA's negligence.

The barrister will explain to the jury the relevant law and how it should be applied in this case.

Claimant's closing speech

Sandra's solicitor now makes the final speech. He explains that the BAA admitted that they were responsible for the lock and that the evidence show that 'in all likelihood' they had not checked it properly to see that it was safe. Unlike a criminal case in the Crown Court, Sandra does not have to prove this so that the judge is sure-it is enough to prove that, on a balance of probabilities the locks were not checked.

He also argues that Sandra should not be blamed for trying to escape when the problem was caused by the negligence of the BAA in the first place.

He describes to the judge what the law is and refers to any relevant cases which have been decided in similar situations, whether they support his case or not. The relevant similar findings are called 'precedents'.

Judgement

The judge now gives his judgement. Usually this happens straightaway but in more complicated cases the judgement can be reserved and given at a later date when the judge has had a chance to consider everything in detail.

In this case, the judge said that this was a simple case. He decided that the BAA were responsible for providing safe changing rooms in the sports centre. He had considered the evidence about checking the locks and that in his view it was more probable than not that this lock hadn't been checked recently. Finally, the judge said that it was reasonable for someone trapped in a cubicle to try to escape provided their efforts were sensible.

The decision was that the BAA should compensate Sandra. However, he also decided that Sandra had been at fault. She had contributed to her own injuries by her own negligence in risking standing on a 'moveable' object-the door handle.

The judge ruled that Sandra's own compensation of £4750 should be reduced by 20% because she had also been at fault. She was therefore awarded £3800.

The above is an outline of a typical county court case. It can be seen, however, that the procedures in the High Courts and country courts have one thing in common. They are bound by formality and involve a set procedure where each party can present their case, either through representatives or on their own behalf, and each can expect to get a full hearing. In the Crown Courts, a jury will, in most cases, make a decision as to innocence and guilt. In the county courts, the judge will do so. However, the processes are similar in many respects.

Summary of trial process in the county court.

1. The claimant or the claimant's solicitor makes an opening speech.
2. The claimant is called to give evidence.
3. The defendant or the defendant's solicitor cross-examines the claimant.
4. There is a re-examination.
5. The defendant or defendant's solicitor makes an opening speech.
6. The defendant gives evidence.
7. There is a cross examination of the defendant.
8. The defendant or defendant's solicitor makes a closing speech.
9. The claimant or claimant's solicitor makes a closing speech.
10. The judge gives his judgement.

Ch. 6

SMALL CLAIMS-AN OVERVIEW OF PROCEDURE

Part 7 of the County Court Rules governs the issue of the claim form. If a defence is not filed, judgement is entered for the claimant because the defendant is in default of the obligation to file a defence. If a defence is filed, the claim is in appropriate circumstances allocated to the small claims track and proceeds under the provisions of Part 27.

The procedure for small claims is informal. The district judge hears the case in a private room although the hearing is now open to the public if they wish to attend, (in practice this is seldom the case). You can claim fixed costs, your own personal costs, witness expenses up to £50 per day, and in certain cases expert fees for reports up to £200 (only if the judge gives permission to use an expert witness). Solicitors' fees are not awarded to the successful party. However, up to £260 may be claimed for legal advice if the claim includes an injunction. You should check these figures at the time of going to court as they are subject to change. This is to encourage members of the public to conduct their own case. The small claims procedure is designed for lawyer-free self-representation.

In certain cases, expenses for travel and overnight accommodation may be claimed. The Court provides standard forms for completion by the opponents throughout a case with the intention that for simple matters, you could present your own case. The same forms are available from the Lord Chancellor's homepage.

Types of Small Claim

Your claim may be for a fixed amount or for an amount to be assessed. In the latter case, liability for the claim is treated separately from assessment of the amount of the claim. In such a case, you would write on the claim form e.g. "not more than £3,000" when the claim is for between £1,000 and £3,000. If a defence is not filed or if such a claim is admitted, you would obtain judgement with damages to be assessed by the district judge at a "disposal hearing". In most cases, you will know the amount of your claim.

Special Features of Part 7 Procedures
- The claimant is entitled to Judgement in default of the defendant filing the Acknowledgement of service and/or the defence, or
- Judgement on liability with damages to be assessed at a disposal hearing

Special features of the Small Claims Track
- Complicated rules do not apply

- The hearing is informal and not in open court although the public can attend.

Completing and Issuing a Claim Form

From 19 March 2012, there was an important change to administration of money claims. If you want to make a county court money claim you must send the claim form to the "County Court Money Claims Centre" (CCMCC) or if you don't want to use the CCMC, then you will have to use Money Claims On-Line (see below). This change was part of improvements to the administration of civil business. Cases will be issued at the CCMCC and where they become defended and ready to be allocated to a track, they will be transferred to an appropriate county court. Claim Forms can be posted to the CCMC at:

Salford Business Centre
PO Box 527
Salford
M5 0BY

Any enquiries on cases proceeding at the CCMCC should be made to the following:

For email enquiries: ccmcccustomerenquiries@hmcts.gov.uk
For e-filing enquiries: ccmcc-filing@hmcts.gov.uk
For telephone enquiries: 0300 1231372
It is important to complete the claim form as accurately as you can. The Claim Form (NI) is shown at the end of this book in

Appendix B. The Claim Form changed when the new CCMC was introduced on 19 March 2012.

Once the claim form has been served on the defendant, permission is needed from the defendant to amend it and if that is not forthcoming then you would have to apply to the court. So ensure you have entered the details correctly and that you have named the defendant correctly. If the defendant is a business then it is important to have the correct legal entity of the organisation. Is the business an incorporated company? If it is, then there should be the word "LTD" or "Limited" after its name. A limited company should have the registered company number on its headed paper and so you can use this number to check the full company name and registered office by visiting Companies House website. It is advisable to state the registered office of a company as the address where the court should send the claim. This should remove any doubts of service. You can of course always send a copy of the claim to the trading address after the court has sent it to the registered office. On the claim form there must be a statement of value. The statement of value should be inserted below the word "Value" on the front page of the claim form. The form of wording should be: "Value: £X plus accrued interest and fixed costs.

In deciding which level of court fee the claim comes within, the court takes into account the interest claimed to the date of the claim.

In a personal injury claim, for example, where you would be claiming general damages for pain and suffering, statement of value would be worded, for example, as " the claimant expects to recover between £5,000 and £15,000".

The particulars of claim must be verified by a statement of truth. The person signing a statement of truth can be guilty of contempt of court if they know that the facts contained within the document are untrue. A solicitor can sign the statement of truth in his own name but states that: "The Claimant believes......". A solicitor should check the contents of the particulars of claim with his client before he signs it on their behalf. If the statement of truth is being signed by an officer of a company, that person must be at a senior level, such as a manager or director.

On the front page of the claim form, there are boxes where you enter the amount of the claim. There is a box for fixed solicitors' costs as allowed by the court rules. These fixed costs can only be claimed if you have a solicitor acting for you.

There is a court fee to issue a court claim. The level of fee depends on the amount claimed. The latest court fees can be obtained from the Court Service website. If a case is defended and progresses to a hearing then there will be further fees to pay. The following shows the further fees payable depending on the track the case is allocated to:

Small Claims Track	Allocation Fee (if over £1,500)	Hearing Fee	
Fast Track	Allocation Fee	Listing Fee	Hearing Fee
Multi Track	Allocation Fee	Listing Fee	Hearing Fee

The current policy of the Ministry of Justice is to make county courts self-financing which has caused a steady increase in court fees. If you are an individual and are either on a qualifying state benefit or your disposable income is below a certain level, you may be able to obtain a full or part fee remission, which means that you will not have to pay all or part of the required court fee. To claim for a "fee remission", you will have to complete the relevant application form and supply up to date documentary evidence regarding your finances. Fee remissions are not available for business. If a claim is issued through the Claim Production Centre, then the court fee is discounted. The Claim Production Centre is designed for those issuing a large number of debt actions.

Freezing Orders

A creditor can prevent a debtor from moving assets out of reach by applying for a freezing order. A freezing order is an injunction which prevents a party from removing assets out of the country or from dealing with the assets. Application for a freezing injunction are usually made to the High Court, but there are exceptions where an order can be granted by a county court such as where it is sought to aid execution after judgment. If you are considering applying for a freezing order, it is strongly recommended that you seek the assistance of a solicitor.

Making a Claim Online

Those with access to the internet can start a claim for money online. To start the claim, you need to visit the Court Service website: www.moneyclaim.gov.uk/web/mcol/welcome

With the introduction of the new County Court Money Claims Centre on 19 March 2012, the use of Money Claim Online is expected to increase. This was probably one of the intentions of introducing a centralised "back office". The issuing of claims online has its attractions. The service is open to individuals, solicitors and companies. It has the advantage that it operates 24 hours a day, 7 days a week and so you can go online anytime and monitor the progress of your case. Also, a change to the court rules that came into force in April 2009 enables more detailed particulars of claim to be served separately within 14 days of issuing the claim. This removed the disadvantage of the online claim form having limited space for giving particulars of the claim. To use "Money Claims Online", the claim has to be for a fixed amount that is less than £100,000. You have to pay for the court fees by credit or debit card. Users of this system cannot obtain an exemption from court fees.

Response Pack

The court will then serve (i.e. post) the claim form on the defendant with a "RESPONSE Pack" containing four forms, a

Form of Acknowledgement, a Form of Admission (N9A), a form for filing a Defence (N9B) and a form for filing a Counterclaim (N9B)

Admitted or Part Admitted Claims: Part 14

The DEFENDANT may either

- Admit/Part admit the claim with an offer to pay immediately. The court will enter judgement.
- Admit/Part admit the claim with an offer to pay in instalments.
- If the claim is part admitted, a defence should be filed to show why part of the claim is not admitted
- If the claim is for an unspecified amount i.e. an amount to be assessed, the defendant can admit the claim and make an offer.

The CLAIMANT may then
- File an application for judgement of the admitted claim
- Accept or reject an offer of instalments on an admitted claim. If you reject the instalments offered, the court clerk will assess the defendant's statement of means and make an order for instalments. If you are dissatisfied with the clerk's decision, you may apply to the district judge for a determination.

- Reject a part admission; in which case the claim proceeds as if defended. And the defendant should file a defence.
- In the case of an admitted claim with the "amount to be assessed", you should apply for judgement to be entered for liability. The court will schedule a "disposal hearing" to determine the amount of the claim or damages payable. If an offer is made in respect of a claim for an unspecified sum, the offer may be either accepted or rejected. If it is rejected, the court will proceed to a "disposal hearing" for damages to be assessed

Refuted Claims

The defendant may as an alternative to admitting the claim:

- File the acknowledgement requesting 28 days to file the defence; or
- File a defence within 14 days; and/or
- File a counterclaim against the claimant; and/or
- Issue a Part 20 Notice against a non-party or a contribution notice against a co-defendant

Judgement in Default

If the defendant does not file a defence within 14 days of the date of service of the claim (or 28 days from filing the acknowledgement of service), the court will at the request of the claimant order judgement in the claimant's favour without a hearing. This is judgement "in default" of the defendant filing a defence. The claimant should file a request for a default judgement after the time period has lapsed. If the amount of the claim is not specified on the claim form, then as indicated above, you should file the request and the court will order judgement for the claimant with damages to be assessed at a disposal hearing.

Defence

The defence is a statement of case and Part 16 requires that it states (a) which allegations in the particulars of claim are denied (b) which are not admitted or denied i.e. that the claimant must prove, and (c) which allegations are admitted. If an allegation is denied, the defendant must (a) state his reason for denying it and (b) if he intends to put forward a different version of events, state his own version. In the case of a defendant who files a Defence, the court will serve a copy on the claimant and the case will be transferred to the defendant's local or "home" court, which will process the claim along the small claims track. If you expect the defendant to file a defence, you will save time if you issue your claim form in his local County Court.

Counterclaim : Part 20

The defendant may make a counterclaim as follows:

- This will be heard with the claim. A court fee will be payable
- If the counterclaim is above the small claims limit of £10,000 the district judge may allocate the claim to a different track.

The defendant's counterclaim is a claim made by the defendant against the claimant, which may be less than his claim, so his claim is reduced, or it may be greater. A counterclaim is a separate action and an alternative to the defendant issuing his own claim form. Both claims are therefore managed in one action or set of proceedings. The defendant is in the same position as the claimant when making a counterclaim. The rules for the content of the counterclaim are the same as for any claim. The claimant must file a defence to the counterclaim to avoid judgement-in-default on the counterclaim. In this respect, the claimant is for the purposes of the counterclaim in the same position as a defendant and the rules governing the content of the defence apply. Counterclaims are dealt with under Part 20. This Part also deals with claims by one defendant against another and circumstances in which a defendant wishes to issue proceedings against a non-party. If you as the defendant to a claim, or a defendant to a counterclaim, consider either to be applicable you should instruct a Solicitor.

Allocation to a Track: Allocation Questionnaire Form

If the defendant files a defence or counterclaim, the Court will:

- Post a form called an "Allocation Questionnaire" (N205A) TO THE PARTIES. This form records the details of the claim, the case number and date of service. The case number is now the reference point for your case and no steps can be taken without quoting it

- Both parties must complete and file the Allocation Questionnaire. The claimant must pay a fee when filing this form.

Directions Issued by the Court

After the Allocation Questionnaire is received, or in default of filing the Allocation Questionnaire, the court will allocate the claim to the small claims track and issue directions. These are the courts instructions as to how the case should proceed. District judges have wide powers to issue directions but for small claims PD27 provides standards form directions depending on the category of claim. The parties may apply for directions using form N244.

Enforcement Proceedings

If the defendant does not comply with a court order or judgement, you must take enforcement proceedings to enforce the judgement.

****

Useful addresses

The Court Services Secretariat
The Lord Chancellors Department
Southside
105 Victoria Street
London SW1E 6QT
Tel: 020 7210 8500
www.lcd.gov.uk

Crown Prosecution Service
Rose Court
2 Southwark Bridge
London SE1 9HS
Tel: 0207 357 0000
www.cps.gov.uk

The Free Representation Unit
Ground Floor
60 Grays Inn road
London WC1X 8LU
Tel: 0207 611 9555
www. thefru.org.uk

The Chartered Institute of Legal Executives
Kempston Manor
Kempston
Bedford MK42 7AB
Tel: 01234 845777 www.cilex.org.uk

The Law Society
113 Chancery lane
London WC2A 1PL
Tel: 020 7242 1222
www.lawsociety.org.uk

Legal Action Group
242 Pentonville Road
London N1 9UN
Tel: 020 7833 8931
www.lag.org.uk

National Association of Citizen Advice Bureaus
115-123 Pentonville Road
London N1 9LZ
Tel: 020 7833 2181
www.citizensadvice.org.uk

Glossary of terms

Acknowledgement of service
Form of reply to, or acknowledgement of, a service of court papers.

Acquittal
Discharge of defendant following verdict or direction of not guilty.

Adjourned generally
Temporary suspension of the hearing of a case by a court for a short period.

Advocate
A barrister or solicitor representing a person in court.

Affidavit
A written statement of evidence on oath or by affirmation to be true.

Appeal
Application to a higher court or authority for a review of a lower court decision.

Appellant
Person who appeals

Attachment of earnings
An order that directs an employer of a debtor to deduct a regular amount from salary or wages to pay off a debt.

Bail
Release of a defendant from custody until his or her appearance in court, usually on the basis of financial security.

Bar
The collective term for barristers

Barrister
A member of the bar, that part of the legal profession that has rights of audience before a judge.

Bench warrant
A warrant issued by a judge for the arrest of an absent defendant.

Bill of indictment
A written statement of the charges against a defendant on trial in the Crown Court and signed by an officer of the court.

Brief
Written instructions to counsel to appear at a hearing of a party prepared by the solicitor and setting out the case and any case law relied upon.

Chambers
Either a private room or court where the public are not allowed and where the judge hears a case or offices used by a barrister.

Circuit judge
A judge who sits in the County and/or High Court.

Civil matters
Matters concerning private rights and not offences of the state.

Claim
Proceedings issued in the County or High Courts which initiate an action.

Claimant
The person issuing the claim, previously known as the plaintiff.

Committal
Committal for trial or sentence or an order to be committed to prison.

Common law
The law established over time by precedent.

Conditional discharge
A discharge of a convicted defendant without sentence on condition that he or she does not re-offend within a period of time.

Co-respondent
A person named as an adulterer (or third person) in a divorce.

Counsel
A Barrister

Counterclaim
A claim made by a defendant against a claimant in a case.

County Court
County courts deal with civil matters including all small claims up to £15,000.

Court of Appeal
Divided into civil and criminal divisions and hears appeals from the High court and the County court.

Crown Court
The Crown Court deals with all crimes committed for judgement to the magistrates court and also hears appeals in cases heard by the magistrates court.

Damages
An amount of money claimed as compensation for physical or material loss e.g. personal injury

Defendant
The person standing trial, the person being sued.

Deposition
A statement of evidence written down and sworn or affirmed.

Determination
The scrutiny of a bill of costs in criminal proceedings in order to determine that the amounts claimed are reasonable.

Discovery of documents
The mutual disclosure of evidence and information held by each side relating to a case.

District judge
A judicial officer of the court.

Exhibit
Item or document referred to in an affidavit or used during the court trial or hearing.

Expert witness
Person employed to give evidence on a subject or matter on which they are knowledgeable and qualified.

Fiat
A decree or command

Garnishee
A summons issued by a claimant against a third party for seizure of money or assets in their keeping.

High Court
A civil court which consists of three divisions, the Queens Bench Division, hearing civil disputes, Family Division concerning matrimonial and child related matters and the Chancery dealing with property and fraud related matters.

Indictable offence
A criminal offence triable only by the Crown Court.

Injunction
An order of the court either restraining a person from carrying out a course of action or directing a course of action to be complied with.

Judge
An officer appointed to administer the law and who has the authority to hear and try cases in a court of law.

Jury
A body of jurors sworn to reach a verdict according to evidence presented in court.

Justice of the peace
A lay-magistrate or person appointed to administer business in a magistrates court. Also sits in the crown court with a judge or a recorder to hear appeals and commute sentences.

Law lords
Describes the judges of the House of Lords.

Legal aid/help
Facility to obtain aid towards fees and expenses relating to court cases.

Libel
A written and published statement/article which contains damaging remarks about another persons character and reputation.

Litigation
Legal proceedings.

Lord Chancellor
The cabinet minister who acts as speaker of the House of Lords and oversees the hearings of the Law Lords. Has other wide responsibilities.

Lord Chief Justice
Senior judge of the Court of Appeal Criminal Division and also heads the Queens Bench Division of the High Courts of Justice.

Magistrates Court
A court where criminal proceedings are commenced. Also has jurisdiction to deal with a range of civil matters.

Master of the Rolls
Senior judge of the Court of Appeal Criminal Division.

Mitigation
Reasons submitted on behalf of a guilty party in order to excuse or partly excuse the offence committed in order to minimise the sentence.

Motion
An application by one party to the High Court for a judgement in their favour.

Notary public
Someone who is authorised to swear oaths and execute deeds.

Oath
A verbal promise by a person of religious beliefs to tell the truth.

Official solicitor
A solicitor or barrister appointed by the Lord Chancellor working in the Lord Chancellors office. The duties include looking after the affairs of people who cannot look after affairs due to incapacity i.e. mental illness.

Oral examination
A method of questioning a person under oath before an officer of the court to obtain details of their financial affairs.

Order
A direction of the court.

Particulars of claim
Details relevant to a case

Party
Any of the participants in a court case.

Penal notice
Directions attached to a court order if breach of that order result in imprisonment.

Personal application
Application made to the court without legal representation.

Plea
A defendants reply to a charge.

Pleadings
Documents setting out the claim or defence of parties involved in legal proceedings.

Precedent
The decision of a case which has established principles and which can be used as authority for a future case.

Pre-trial review

A preliminary appointment at which the district judge examines the issues and issues directions and a timetable for the case.

Queens Counsel

Barristers of at least ten years standing, they take on work of importance and are know as 'Silks'.

Recorder

Members of the legal profession (barristers or solicitors) who are appointed to act in a senior capacity on a part time basis and who may progress to the post of full time judge.

Registrar

Known now as district judge and deputy district judges they are active in the county courts.

Right of audience

Entitlement to appear in front of a court in a legal capacity and conduct proceedings.

Solicitor

Member of the legal profession chiefly concerned with representing clients and preparing cases.

Summary judgement

Judgement obtained from the claimant where there is no defence or no valid grounds for defence.

Summing up

A review of the evidence by representatives of the claimant and defendant before the jury retires to give its verdict.

Tort

A civil wrong committed against a person for which compensation may be sought.

Verdict

The finding of guilty or not guilty by a jury.

Witness

A person who gives evidence to court.

Index

Appendix One

Court Charters for:

Magistrates Court
Crown Court
Family Court
Royal Courts of Justice

Courts Charter - Magistrates' Courts

This leaflet sets out the standard of service you can expect from any Magistrates' Court in England and Wales in relation to Criminal work. We have set these standards after talking to people who have used the court. We aim to provide an excellent, courteous service and when you come to court you can expect fair and equal treatment, no matter what your age, ethnic origin, sexual orientation, disability, gender or religious beliefs.

This Charter is about the administration of the court and not the decisions made by magistrates. You may be able to appeal to a higher court if you are unhappy about the outcome of your case. If you want to do so you should obtain legal advice. Please note that court staff are unable to give legal advice to customers.

If you are coming to court

When you are first asked to come to court, we, the prosecution or defence will provide:

- a map of how to get to court;
- details of public transport and any car parks near the court;
- details of the times the court is open;
- information on the availability of refreshments, telephones, separate waiting areas etc;
- the contact details of the Customer Service or appropriate Court Officer.

Before the date of your hearing you can:

- ask to visit a court room;
- ask us to arrange seats in the court room or public gallery (if we can) for anyone who comes to your hearing with you. However, this is not always possible. For example in the youth court only the parent or guardian and solicitor are allowed in the hearing.

If you require an interpreter for the court hearing please inform the Listings Officer immediately as soon as you know your hearing date. If you have a disability and need help at your court hearing, please speak to the Customer Service or Disabled Persons Officer who will tell you how we can help you.

Please note that smoking is strictly prohibited in any part of our buildings.

The magistrates' court will often have a separate "Admin Centre" or "Fixed Penalty Unit" to the courthouse. At the courthouse there is normally an enquiry point open from 9am on days when there are hearings. The public counter in the Admin Centre is normally open from 10am to 4pm although locally some may be open for longer than this national minimum standard.

When you visit you will find:

- courteous, polite, helpful staff wearing identity badges;
- clear signs to help you find your way around;
- a duty solicitor is generally available for defendants who are eligible for this assistance when a criminal court is sitting;
- information leaflets on display and a list of adult criminal cases to be heard that day;
- a notice giving details of the Customer Service Officer or Courthouse Manager who will be pleased to help you with any special needs, suggestions or complaints.

When you go to the public counter or enquiry point we will:

- respect your privacy;
- talk to you out of the hearing of other members of the public, if you prefer;
- use simple clear language and ensure all technical terms are explained;
- attend to your enquiry within 10 minutes or explain the delay if you have to wait longer.

You can contact us by phone Monday to Friday between 9am and 5pm and we will:

- answer the phone promptly and helpfully;
- give the name of the person you are speaking to;
- give you a clear and helpful answer;
- ensure that if the office is closed for any reason an answerphone will take your message and we will return your call the next working day.

When you write to the court, and we need to reply, we will:

- write to you or phone you within 10 working days of receiving your letter;
- tell you who is writing and provide a phone number to contact them if you wish.

Court hearings

Hearings are arranged as quickly as possible and for criminal "charge" cases we aim to:

- have no more than 5 working days between the start of proceedings against an adult and the first appearance in court;
- have no more than 7 working days between the start of proceedings against a youth and the first appearance in a youth court.

For "summons" cases we aim for the hearing to be arranged for no more than 28 working days between issue of the summons and the first appearance in court.

If we have to change the date of your hearing, we will let you know as soon as possible.

We will arrange hearings to prevent contact between youth and adult proceedings and family and criminal cases wherever possible.

Waiting at court

You shouldn't have to wait more than 1 hour from the time you are asked to attend to when you are called to give evidence. However, delays are sometimes unavoidable, for example if the case before yours takes longer than planned.

If you have to wait we will ensure that:

- you are told regularly how much longer you may have to wait and the reason for the delay;
- you are told as quickly as possible, through the people who called you as a witness, if your case cannot be heard that day.

For witnesses we will also seek to:

- provide separate waiting areas where possible;
- consider arrangements for you to wait apart from other parties if there isn't a separate area. Please ask the court staff if you would prefer this.

Our service for child and vulnerable / intimidated adult witnesses

We know that giving evidence in court can be very difficult and stressful for a child or vulnerable / intimidated adult witness so we will:

- arrange to have any case involving a child or vulnerable / intimidated adult witness heard as soon as possible;
- ensure the Witness Service or other support agency meets children and their companions or vulnerable / intimidated adults when they come to court and takes them to a private waiting area away from the defendant;
- explain how we do things in court and answer any questions.

The judge, magistrate or district judge may let such witnesses give evidence using a Video Link. If they do, we can arrange for the witness to see the room and how the equipment works before the trial. If you want to know whether a Video Link may be used, please ask the solicitors involved in your case. Applications for such "special measures" are made formally in advance of the trial.

Witness Service

The Witness Service is run by the independent charity, Victim Support, and helps victims, prosecution and defence witnesses and their families before, during and after the hearing. Trained volunteers in every magistrate and youth court give free and confidential support and practical information about how we do things in court. They will not offer an opinion on the case or discuss the crime. They will normally get in touch with you before the court hearing to offer their help.

The help they offer includes:

- arranging a visit to court before the hearing;
- arranging for someone to go into the court room with you if you have to give evidence;
- giving you the chance to talk over the case after it's ended and advising where to get more help or information.

If you would like help, or if you'd like to volunteer for the Witness Service, you can contact them at:

Victim Support National Office,
Cranmer House,
39 Brixton Road,
London SW9 6DZ

Telephone: 020 7735 9166
email: contact@victimsupport.org.uk
website: www.victimsupport.org.uk

At court you will probably come into contact with people from the police, National Probation Service and Crown Prosecution Service. Although we aren't responsible for the services they provide, you may get information about them from the court.

Crown Prosecution Service

This organisation decides if crimes investigated by the police should go to court. If they do, the CPS is responsible for the prosecution case. You can contact them at:

Crown Prosecution Service,
50 Ludgate Hill,
London EC4M 7EX

Telephone: 020 7796 8000
email: enquiries@cps.gsi.gov.uk
website: www.cps.gov.uk

Authorities such as the HM Revenue & Customs can also bring prosecutions. Please ask our staff for more details.

National Probation Service

National Probation Directorate,
1st Floor,
Abell House,
John Islip Street,
London SW1P 4LH
email: npd.publicenquiry@homeoffice.gsi.gov.uk
website: www.probation.homeoffice.gov.uk

If you are a defendant

If you are on bail, and you require it, we will send you or your solicitor a copy of this Charter.

If you don't have a solicitor and require an interpreter for the court hearing please inform the Listings Officer at the court as soon as you know your hearing date.

If you cannot hear very well and you need help at your court hearing, or if you have any other special needs, please speak to the Customer Service, or Listings Officer who will tell you how we can help you.

We try to arrange hearings as quickly as possible. We are trying to reduce delays, but many things can affect how soon we can arrange the hearing, so we cannot guarantee when your case will be heard. We do give priority to hearings for defendants in custody.

Criminal Defence Service

You may be able to get legal aid to help pay your legal fees for representation. You can find out by contacting:

The Legal Services Commission,
85 Grays Inn Road,
London WC1X 8TX

Telephone: 020 7759 0000
email addresses for regional offices are on their website: www.legalservices.gov.uk

Community Legal Service

CLS Direct, a free government funded service, will provide information on where you can obtain the type of legal advice you need.

Telephone: 0845 345 4345
website: www.clsdirect.org.uk

Citizens Advice Bureau

The CAB gives free, confidential, impartial and independent advice on a wide range of subjects. The phone number and address of the local office will be displayed in the court.

website: www.citizensadvice.org.uk

Listening to you

We welcome your comments and suggestions on how we could improve our service to you. We do this by:

- inviting you to fill in comment cards;
- carrying out local surveys;
- paying attention to all comments, complaints and suggestions;
- displaying information about our performance;
- displaying details in court waiting areas of complaints and suggestions and what we have done to make improvements as a result of your feedback;
- displaying results of local surveys and changes we have made because of them.

If you have a complaint, please tell us as soon as possible and we will do our best to sort out the problem there and then. If you are still not happy, you can speak to the Customer Service Officer or Courthouse Manager. If you prefer, you can write to the Courthouse Manager of the court in question.

We aim to resolve and respond to the complaint, giving you a full answer within 5 working days of receipt.

A leaflet called "I want to complain – what should I do" is available in every court. For more information please ask one of the court staff or visit our website at:

www.hmcourts-service.gov.uk

We welcome suggestions and compliments too.

Whilst we can investigate complaints about how a magistrate or judge behaved in court we cannot investigate anything to do with their judgment, their assessment of a case or overturn any of their decisions.

Information about how to make a complaint about the personal conduct of magistrates and judges is available on the web:

www.judicialcomplaints.gov.uk

Such complaints about a judge may be sent in writing to:

Office for Judicial Complaints (OJC),
4th Floor, Clive House,
70 Petty France,
London SW1H 9HD

Complaints about the personal conduct of magistrates should be sent in writing to your local Advisory Committee. You can find details of your local Advisory Committee by asking at the court office or by visiting the website on:

www.dca.gov.uk/magistrates/docs/advisorycomslist.pdf

Letters to the OJC or Advisory Committee should include the name of the judge or magistrate and court, your case number and hearing date together with the specific details of the conduct about which you are complaining.

Although we cannot look into complaints about solicitors, barristers or any other organisation, you may find the following addresses useful:

Solicitors

Consumer Complaints Service,
The Law Society,
Victoria Court,
8 Dormer Place,
Leamington Spa,
Warwickshire CV32 5AE

Helpline: 0845 608 6565
Textphone: 0845 601 1682
Fax: 01926 431435
email: enquiries@lawsociety.org.uk
website: www.oss.lawsociety.org.uk

Barristers

If you would like a complaint form please write to:

The Complaints Department,
The General Council of the Bar,
Northumberland House,
289-293 High Holborn,
London WC1V 7HZ

Telephone: 020 7242 0082
Fax: 020 7611 1342
email: complaints@barcouncil.org.uk
website: www.barcouncil.org.uk

Police

Independent Police Complaints Commission (IPCC),
90 High Holborn,
London WC1V 6BH

Telephone: 08453 002 002
email: enquires@ipcc.gsi.gov.uk
website: www.ipcc.gov.uk

Courts Charter - The Crown Court

This leaflet sets out the standard of service you can expect from any Crown Court in England and Wales. We have set these standards after talking to people who have used the court. We aim to provide an excellent, courteous service and when you come to court you can expect fair and equal treatment, no matter what your age, ethnic origin, sexual orientation, disability, gender or religious beliefs.

This Charter is about the administration of the court and not the decisions made by judges. Appeal procedures against decisions of the court are available to the prosecution and defence. Please note that court staff are unable to give legal advice to customers.

If you are coming to court

When you are first asked to come to court, we, the prosecution or the defence will provide:

- a map of how to get to court;
- details of public transport and any car parks near the court;
- details of the times the court is open;
- information on the availability of refreshments, telephones, separate waiting areas etc;
- the contact details of the Customer Service or appropriate Court Officer.

Before the date of your hearing you can

- ask to visit a court room;
- ask us to arrange seats in the court room or public gallery (if we can) for anyone who comes to your hearing with you.

If you have a disability and need help at your court hearing, please speak to the Customer Service Officer who will tell you how we can help you.

Please note that smoking is strictly prohibited in any part of our buildings.

The court building is normally open from 9am on days when there are hearings. The public counter or enquiry point is open from 10am to 4pm although locally some may be open for longer than this national minimum standard.

When you come to court you will find:

- courteous, polite, helpful staff wearing identity badges;
- clear signs to help you find your way around;
- information leaflets on display and a list of cases to be heard that day;
- a notice giving details of the Customer Service Officer or Court Manager who will be pleased to help you with any special needs, suggestions or complaints.

When you go to the public counter or enquiry point we will:

- respect your privacy;
- talk to you out of the hearing of other members of the public, if you prefer;
- use simple clear language and ensure all technical terms are explained;
- attend to your enquiry within 10 minutes or explain the delay if you have to wait longer.

You can contact us by phone Monday to Friday between 9am and 5pm and we will:

- answer the phone promptly and helpfully;
- give the name of the person you are speaking to;
- give you a clear and helpful answer.

When you write to the court, and we need to reply, we will:

- write to you or phone you within 10 working days of receiving your letter;
- tell you who is writing and provide a phone number to contact them if you wish.

Being a juror

If we ask you to be a juror we will:

- send you a jury summons at least 4 weeks before we need you;
- tell you how to apply to have your jury service deferred or to apply to be excused.

We will also send you:

- a booklet (Your Guide to Jury Service) about your duties as a juror;
- a leaflet explaining the allowances you can claim;
- a leaflet with a map of how to get to court, details of public transport and any car parks near the court;
- details of the times the court is open;
- information on the availability of refreshments, telephones, separate waiting areas etc;
- details on how to contact the court.

When you arrive at court we will:

- show you to a separate waiting area;
- show you a video giving you more details about being a juror;
- make sure one of our staff is available to answer your questions;
- respect your privacy and talk to you in private if you prefer;
- tell you how many days you can expect to sit as a juror.

How we use your time

Although we only summons the number of jurors we need, changes in circumstances mean that you may not be called upon as a juror in a trial for every day of your jury service. Nevertheless we aim to use your time as efficiently as possible.

While you are waiting to sit on a trial we will:

- tell you at least every hour when you're likely to be needed in court;
- let you go as soon as possible if your services are not needed.

We will also:

- let you return to work on days, or part days, if you aren't needed (if your employer agrees);
- give you a special phone number to call (in our larger Crown Court centres) to find out if you need to come to court that day;
- explain how (in our smaller courts) we make sure you know when you need to come into court.

When you are selected for a jury, you will have to swear an oath or make an affirmation (declaration) when you go into the courtroom. We will display the words of the most common oaths and the affirmation in the jury waiting area for you to read in advance.

Court hearings

Hearings are arranged as quickly as possible, but whilst we aim to keep delays to a minimum, many things can affect how soon a case will be given a date for hearing.

Although we cannot guarantee when your case will be heard we aim to:

- have the first hearing within 7 weeks from when we receive your case;
- start most trials within 16 weeks of when we receive the case.

If you are a witness

If the date of your case is delayed you can ask us to:

- explain the delay, or tell you who can explain it to you;
- tell you when your case is likely to be heard.

If we have to change the date of your hearing, we will let the prosecution or defence who called you as a witness, know as soon as possible.

Waiting at court

You shouldn't have to wait more than 2 hours from the time you are asked to attend to when you are called to give evidence. However, delays are sometimes unavoidable, for example if the case before yours takes longer than planned.

If you have to wait we will ensure that:

- you are told regularly how much longer you may have to wait and the reason for the delay;
- you are told as quickly as possible, through the people who called you as a witness, if your case cannot be heard that day.

For witnesses we will also seek to:

- provide separate waiting areas where possible;
- consider arrangements for you to wait apart from other parties if there isn't a separate area. Please ask the court staff if you would prefer this.

Our service for child and vulnerable / intimidated adult witnesses

We know that giving evidence in court can be very difficult and stressful for a child or vulnerable / intimidated adult witness so we will:

- arrange to have any case involving a child or vulnerable / intimidated adult witness heard as soon as possible;
- ensure the Witness Service or other support agency meets children and their companions or vulnerable / intimidated adults when they come to court and takes them to a private waiting area away from the defendant;
- explain how we do things in court and answer any questions.

The judge may let such witnesses give evidence using a Video Link. If they do, we can arrange for the witness to see the room and how the equipment works before the trial. If you want to know whether a Video Link may be used, please ask the solicitors involved in your case. Applications for such "special measures" are made formally in advance of the trial.

Witness Service

The Witness Service is run by the independent charity, Victim Support, and helps victims, prosecution and defence witnesses and their families before, during and after the hearing. Trained volunteers in every crown court centre give free and confidential support and practical information about how we do things in court. They will not offer an opinion on the case or discuss the crime. They will normally get in touch with you before the court hearing to offer their help.

The help they offer includes:

- arranging a visit to court before the hearing;
- arranging for someone to go into the court room with you if you have to give evidence;
- giving you the chance to talk over the case after it's ended and advising where to get more help or information.

If you would like help, or if you'd like to volunteer for the Witness Service, you can contact them at:

Victim Support National Office,
Cranmer House,
39 Brixton Road,
London SW9 6DZ

Telephone: 020 7735 9166
email: contact@victimsupport.org.uk
website: www.victimsupport.org.uk

Travel expenses and allowances

If you are a juror or a defence witness of fact you can claim travel expenses and allowances.

If you are a prosecution witness you should get your claim form from the prosecuting authority. They will:

- explain what expenses and allowances you can claim;
- give you a reply-paid envelope in which to return your completed form.

If you are a witness, you may be able to claim your expenses and allowances immediately after you have given evidence. We will:

- tell you if you can do this;
- if you cannot, we will tell you why not.

We will pay witness expenses within 5 days of receipt and jurors expenses within 5 days of the conclusion of their service or within 5 days of the conclusion of the first 2 weeks of service.

If you are a defendant found not guilty at your trial, and the judge agrees, you may be able to claim travel expenses, normally with the assistance of your solicitor. However, you won't be able to claim for loss of earnings. We will:

- give you a claim form and help you fill it in;
- send you the money within 5 working days from when we receive your claim form.

If you are a defendant

If you are on bail, and you require it, we will send you or your solicitor a copy of this charter.

If you don't have a solicitor and require an interpreter for the court hearing please inform the Listings Officer at the court as soon as you know your hearing date. If you cannot hear very well and you need help at your court hearing, or if you have any other special needs, please speak to the Customer Service or Listings Officer who will tell you how we can help you.

We try to arrange hearings as quickly as possible. We are trying to reduce delays, but many things can affect how soon we can arrange trials, so we cannot guarantee when your case will be heard. We do give priority to trials for defendants in custody.

If you have been committed from the magistrates' court to the crown court to be sentenced we aim to sentence you within 10 weeks from when we receive your case.

Appeals

If you are appealing against a decision in the magistrates' court, we aim to:

- deal with the appeal within 14 weeks of receiving it;
- if it takes longer than 14 weeks, we will tell you the reason for the delay if you ask us.

At court you will probably come into contact with people from the Police, National Probation Service and Crown Prosecution Service. Although we aren't responsible for the services they provide, you can get information about them from the court.

Crown Prosecution Service

This organisation decides if crimes investigated by the police should go to court. If they do, the CPS is responsible for the prosecution case.

You can contact them at:

Crown Prosecution Service,
50 Ludgate Hill,
London EC4M 7EX

Telephone: 020 7796 8000
email: enquires@cps.gsi.gov.uk
website: www.cps.gov.uk

Authorities such as the HM Revenue and Customs can also bring prosecutions. Please ask our staff for more details.

National Probation Service

National Probation Directorate,
1st Floor, Abell House,
John Islip Street,
London SW1P 4LH

email: npd.publicenquiry@homeoffice.gsi.gov.uk
website: www.probation.homeoffice.gov.uk

Criminal Defence Service

You may be able to get legal aid to help pay your legal fees for representation. You can find out by contacting:

The Legal Services Commission,
85 Grays Inn Road,
London WC1X 8TX

Telephone: 020 7759 0000
email addresses for regional offices are on their website: www.legalservices.gov.uk

Community Legal Service

CLS Direct, a free government funded service, will provide information on where you can obtain the type of legal advice you need.

Telephone: 0845 345 4345
website: www.clsdirect.org.uk

Listening to you

We welcome your comments and suggestions on how we could improve our service to you. We do this by:

- inviting you to fill in comment cards;
- carrying out local surveys;
- paying attention to all comments, complaints and suggestions;
- displaying information about our performance;
- displaying details in court waiting areas of complaints and suggestions and what we have done to make improvements as a result of your feedback;
- displaying results of local surveys and changes we have made because of them.

If you have a complaint, please tell us as soon as possible and we will do our best to sort out the problem there and then. If you are still not happy, you can speak to the Customer Service Officer or the Court Manager. If you prefer, you can write to the Court Manager of the court in question.

We aim to resolve and respond to the complaint, giving you a full answer within 5 working days of receipt.

A leaflet called "I want to complain – what should I do" is also available in every court. For more information please ask one of the court staff or visit our website at:

www.hmcourts-service.gov.uk

We welcome suggestions and compliments too.

Whilst we can investigate complaints about how a judge behaved in court we cannot investigate anything to do with their judgment, their assessment of a case or overturn any of their decisions.

Information about how to make a complaint about the personal conduct of judges is available on the web:

www.judicialcomplaints.gov.uk

Such complaints may be sent in writing to:

Office for Judicial Complaints (OJC),
4th Floor, Clive House,
70 Petty France,
London SW1H 9HD

Telephone: 020 7189 2937
Fax: 020 7189 2936

Your letter should include the name of the judge and court, your case number and hearing date together with the specific details of the conduct about which you are complaining.

Although we cannot look into complaints about solicitors, barristers or any other organisation, you may find the following addresses useful:

Solicitors

Consumer Complaints Service,
The Law Society,
Victoria Court, 8 Dormer Place,
Leamington Spa,
Warwickshire CV32 5AE

Helpline: 0845 608 6565
Textphone: 0845 601 1682
Fax: 01926 431435
email: enquiries@lawsociety.org.uk
website: www.oss.lawsociety.org.uk

Barristers

If you would like a complaint form please write to:

The Complaints Department,
The General Council of the Bar,
Northumberland House,
289-293 High Holborn,
London WC1V 7HZ

Telephone: 020 7242 0082
Fax: 020 7611 1342
email: complaints@barcouncil.org.uk
website: www.barcouncil.org.uk

Police

Independent Police Complaints Commission (IPCC),
90 High Holborn,
London WC1V 6BH

Telephone: 08453 002 002
email: enquires@ipcc.gsi.gov.uk
website: www.ipcc.gov.uk

Courts Charter - Family Courts

This leaflet sets out the standard of service you can expect from any Family (County or Magistrates) Court in England and Wales. We have set these standards after talking to people who have used the court. We aim to provide an excellent, courteous service and when you come to court you can expect fair and equal treatment, no matter what your age, ethnic origin, sexual orientation, disability, gender or religious beliefs.

This Charter is about the administration of the court and not the decisions made by judges or magistrates. You may be able to appeal to a higher court if you are unhappy about the outcome of your case. If you want to do so you should get legal advice. Please note that court staff are unable to give legal advice to customers.

If you are coming to court

When you are first asked to come to court we will send you, or your solicitor:

- a map of how to get to court;
- details of public transport and any car parks near the court;
- details of the times the court is open;
- information on the availability of refreshments, telephones, separate waiting areas etc;
- the contact details of the Customer Service Officer or appropriate Court Officer.

Before the date of your hearing you can ask to see the type of room, or court, where your case will be heard. The use of video conferencing facilities is also available with the court's permission. A list of video conferencing sites is available on the HMCS website or from your local Care Centre.

If you have a disability and need help at your court hearing, please speak to the Customer Service or Disabled Persons Officer who will tell you how we can help you.

We can provide foreign language interpreters for some types of case but for others you will need to arrange and pay for this yourself. The court staff will provide further information on request.

The court building is normally open from 9am on days when there are hearings. The public counter or enquiry point is normally open from 10am to 4pm although locally some may be open for longer than this national minimum standard.

Please note that smoking is strictly prohibited in any part of our buildings.

When you come to court you will find:

- courteous, polite, helpful staff wearing identity badges;
- clear signs to help you find your way around;
- information leaflets on display;
- a notice giving the details of the Customer Service Officer or Courthouse Manager who will be pleased to help you with any special needs, suggestions or complaints.

When you go to the public counter or enquiry point we will:

- respect your privacy;
- talk to you out of the hearing of other members of the public, if you prefer;
- use simple clear language and ensure all technical terms are explained;
- attend to your enquiry within 10 minutes or explain the delay if you have to wait longer.

You can contact us by phone Monday to Friday between 9am and 5pm and we will:

- answer the phone promptly and helpfully;
- give the name of the person you are speaking to;
- give you a clear and helpful answer;
- ensure that if the office is closed for any reason an answerphone will take your message and we will return your call the next working day.

When you write to the court, and we need to reply, we will:

- write to you or phone you within 10 working days of receiving your letter;
- tell you who is writing and provide a phone number to contact them if you wish.

If you want to start a case we will:

- send out the documents relating to your case within 10 working days from receipt of your request;
- tell you the reference number of your case within 10 working days of your case being commenced;
- tell you the date you must come to court if this is appropriate.

We can give you forms and offer guidance on how to complete them but we cannot give you legal advice or tell you what to say. We won't be able to say if your case is likely to succeed, or tell you what the court will decide.

We can tell you how to get advice from a solicitor, the Citizens Advice Bureau or other relevant agencies.

Community Legal Service

CLS Direct, a free government funded service, will provide information on where you can obtain the type of legal advice you need.

Telephone: 0845 345 4345
website: www.clsdirect.org.uk

Citizens Advice Bureau

The CAB gives free, confidential, impartial and independent advice on a wide range of subjects. The phone number and address of the local office will be displayed in the court.

website: www.citizensadvice.org.uk

Your court hearing

Most family cases are heard in private. If you are worried or have any concerns about the arrangements we have made for your case, please speak to one of the court staff who can advise on the availability of special facilities.

If your case has to go to court, we cannot guarantee when it will be heard. However, we aim:

- to list a case for directions, a first appointment or mediation within 6 weeks from the first application;
- to have a case completed within 40 weeks from the first appointment to final order;
- to have a case for adoption completed within 20 weeks from the first appointment to final order;
- to list a case for the first ancillary relief hearing within 16 weeks from the application.

When you arrive at court we will:

- show on a notice board where your case will be heard;
- arrange for you to wait apart from the other side's witnesses if there is no separate area. Please ask the court staff if you would prefer this;
- deal with your case as soon as possible. However, delays can happen, for example if the case before yours takes longer than planned.

If you have to wait we will:

- tell you regularly how much longer you may have to wait;
- tell you as quickly as possible if your case cannot be heard that day.

If we have to change the date of your hearing we will let you know as soon as we can.

Court decisions and orders

The judge or magistrate may hear your case in court or make a decision based on the documents relating to your case. We will send you an order setting out the courts decision within 10 working days from the date the decision was made.

If you and the other people involved in your case prepare the order, we will send it out within 10 working days from the date we receive the documents.

Divorce / Dissolution

If you ask us to issue a *divorce / dissolution petition*, we will send a copy to your husband, wife or civil partner, and anyone else who should get a copy, within 10 working days.

If the court decides you should have a divorce / dissolution, we will send you, and your husband, wife or civil partner, a *decree nisi* (the court order leading to a divorce / dissolution). We will do this within 10 working days from the date the court makes the decision.

You can apply for your decree absolute 6 weeks and one day from the date your decree nisi was pronounced. We will then:

- send out a *decree absolute* (divorce / dissolution court order) on the day we get your application and fee;
- hand you the decree absolute if you come to the court to collect it.

Parental Responsibility Agreement

These forms can be obtained from any family court. Once you have taken your completed *parental responsibility agreement* to the family court it will be registered within 7 working days from when it is received.

How to get more information

If you want to find out about the Children Act 1989 and other children's issues, you can get information from the

Department of Health,
PO Box 777,
London SE1 6XH

website: www.doh.gov.uk

Leaflets on various aspects of family cases are available from any family court. We will send you the leaflets you ask for within 10 days. They are also available on our website:

www.hmcourts-service.gov.uk

Listening to you

We welcome your comments and suggestions on how we could improve our service to you. We do this by:

- inviting you to fill in comment cards;
- carrying out local surveys;
- paying attention to all comments, complaints and suggestions;
- displaying information about our performance;
- displaying details in court waiting areas of complaints and suggestions and what we have done to make improvements as a result of your feedback;
- displaying results of local surveys and changes we have made because of them.

If you have a complaint, please tell us as soon as possible and we will do our best to sort out the problem there and then. If you're still not happy, you can speak to the Customer Service Officer or Family Manager. If you prefer, you can write to the Court Manager of the court in question.

We aim to resolve and respond to the complaint, giving you a full answer within 5 working days of receipt.

A leaflet called "I want to complain – what should I do" is available in every court. For more information please ask one of the court staff or visit our website at:

www.hmcourts-service.gov.uk

We welcome suggestions and compliments too.

Whilst we can investigate complaints about how a magistrate or judge behaved in court we cannot investigate anything to do with their judgment, their assessment of a case or overturn any of their decisions. Information about how to make a complaint about the personal conduct of magistrates and judges is available on the web:

www.judicialcomplaints.gov.uk

Such complaints about the personal conduct of judges in the County Court should be sent to:

Office for Judicial Complaints (OJC),
4th Floor, Clive House,
70 Petty France,
London SW1H 9HD

Telephone: 020 7189 2937
Fax: 020 7189 2936

Complaints about the personal conduct of magistrates in the Family Proceedings Court should be sent in writing to your local Advisory Committee. You can find details of your local Advisory Committee by asking at the court office or by visiting the website on:

www.dca.gov.uk/magistrates/docs/advisorycomslist.pdf

Your letter to the OJC or the Advisory Committee should include the name of the judge or magistrate and court, your case number and hearing date together with the specific details of the conduct about which you are complaining.

Although we cannot look into complaints about solicitors, barristers or any other organisation, you may find the following addresses useful:

Solicitors

Consumer Complaints Service,
The Law Society,
Victoria Court,
8 Dormer Place,
Leamington Spa,
Warwickshire CV32 5AE

Helpline: 0845 608 6565
Textphone: 0845 601 1682
Fax: 01926 431435
email: enquiries@lawsociety.org.uk
website: www.oss.lawsociety.org.uk

Barristers

If you would like a complaint form please write to:

The Complaints Department,
The General Council of the Bar,
Northumberland House,
289-293 High Holborn,
London WC1V 7HZ

Telephone: 020 7242 0082
Fax: 020 7611 1342
email: complaints@barcouncil.org.uk
website: www.barcouncil.org.uk

Courts Charter - The Royal Courts of Justice

This leaflet sets out the standard of service you can expect from The Royal Courts of Justice. We have set these standards after talking to people who have used the court. We aim to provide an excellent, courteous service and when you come to court you can expect fair and equal treatment, no matter what your age, ethnic origin, sexual orientation, disability, gender or religious beliefs.

This Charter is about the administration of the court and not the decisions made by judges. You may be able to appeal to a higher court if you are unhappy about the outcome of your case. If you want to do so you should get legal advice. Please note that court staff are unable to give legal advice to customers.

If you are coming to court

Before the date of your hearing you can ask to see the type of room, or court, where your case will be heard.

If you have a disability and you need help at your court hearing, please let us know in advance by speaking to a Customer Service Officer who will tell you how we can help you.

Please tell the Criminal Appeal Office if you need a foreign language interpreter for a criminal appeal and we will arrange one. We don't normally provide an interpreter for any other matter and you will need to arrange and pay for this yourself. The List Office for your case will tell you who you should contact if you need one.

The main building is open from 9am. The public counters or enquiry points are open from 10am to 4.30pm. Please note that smoking is strictly prohibited in any part of our buildings.

When you come to court you will find:

- courteous, polite, helpful staff wearing identity badges;
- clear signs to help you find your way around;
- information leaflets on display and a list of cases to be heard that day;
- a notice giving details of the Customer Service Officers who will be pleased to help you with any special needs, suggestions or complaints.

When you go to a public counter or enquiry point we will:

- respect your privacy;
- talk to you out of the hearing of other members of the public, if you prefer;
- use simple clear language and ensure all technical terms are explained;
- attend to your enquiry within 10 minutes or explain the delay if you have to wait longer.

You can contact us by phone Monday to Friday between 9am and 5pm and we will:

- answer the phone promptly and helpfully;
- give the name of the person you are speaking to;
- give you a clear and helpful answer.

When you write to the court, and we need to reply, we will:

- write to you or phone you within 10 working days of receiving your letter;
- tell you who is writing and provide a phone number to contact them if you wish.

If you want to start a case we will:

- send out the documents relating to your case within 10 working days from receipt of your request;
- tell you the reference number of your case within 10 working days of the case being commenced;
- tell you the date you must come to court if this is appropriate.

We can give you forms and offer guidance on how to complete them but we cannot give you legal advice or tell you what to say. We won't be able to say if your case is likely to succeed, or tell you what the court will decide.

We can tell you how to get advice from a solicitor, Citizens Advice Bureau or other relevant agencies.

Legal Aid

You should ask the Registrar of Criminal Appeals or the Criminal Appeal Office at The Royal Courts of Justice for information on legal aid in the Court of Appeal Criminal Division.

For other matters you can find out if you may be able to get legal aid to help pay your legal fees for representation by contacting:

The Legal Services Commission,
85 Grays Inn Road,
London WC1X 8TX

Telephone: 020 7759 0000
website: www.legalservices.gov.uk

Community Legal Service

CLS Direct, a free government funded service, will provide information on where you can obtain the type of legal advice you need.

Telephone: 0845 345 4345
website: www.clsdirect.org.uk

Personal Support Unit

The PSU is an independent charity that provides a trained group of volunteers who support litigants in person, witnesses or victims of crime and their families and friends. They can accompany clients to court or around the building and offers both practical and emotional support. The PSU cannot give legal advice or fill in forms for clients.

There is an office in The Royal Courts of Justice. Please ask at reception for further information.

Telephone: 0207 947 7701
website: www.thepsu.co.uk

Citizens Advice Bureau

The CAB gives free, confidential, impartial and independent advice on a wide range of subjects, including debt, benefits, housing, legal matters, employment, immigration and consumer issues. There is a branch of the Citizens Advice Bureau in the Royal Courts of Justice,

RCJ Advice Bureau,
Room M27,
The Royal Courts of Justice,
Strand,
London WC2A 2LL

Telephone Advice Line: 0845 1203715
(recorded message)
website: www.rcjadvice.org.uk

You can also contact the CAB regional office at:

Citizens Advice,
Myddelton House,
115-123 Pentonville Road,
London N1 9LZ

website: www.citizensadvice.org.uk

Your Court hearing

When you arrive at Court we will:

- show on a notice board where your case will be heard;
- arrange for you to wait apart from the other side's witnesses if there is no separate area. Please ask the court if you would prefer this;
- deal with your case as soon as possible. However, delays can happen, for example if the case before yours takes longer than planned.

If you have to wait we will:

- tell you regularly how much longer you may have to wait;
- tell you as quickly as possible if your case cannot be heard that day.

If we have to change the date of your hearing we will let you know as soon as possible.

Court decisions and orders

The judge may hear your case in court or make a decision based on the documents relating to your case. We will send you an order setting out the courts decision within 10 working days from the date the decision was made.

If you and the other people involved in your case, or your legal representatives, have drawn up the order in your case then we will seal and send the order back to you. We will do this within 10 working days from the day we receive it.

Listening to you

We welcome your comments and suggestions on how we could improve our service to you. We do this by:

- inviting you to fill in comment cards;
- carrying out local surveys;
- paying attention to all comments, complaints and suggestions;
- displaying information about our performance;
- displaying details in Court waiting areas of complaints and suggestions and what we have done to make improvements as a result of your feedback;
- displaying results of local surveys and changes we have made because of them.

If you have a complaint, please tell us as soon as possible and we will do our best to sort out the problem there and then. If you are still not happy, you can speak to a Customer Service Officer or write to the relevant Court Manager. We aim to resolve and respond to the complaint, giving you a full answer within 5 working days of receipt.

If you are still dissatisfied with the response given you may write to the appropriate Area Director at the Royal Courts of Justice, Strand, London WC2A 2LL as follows:

The High Court Director's Office,
Room TM 8.12
Telephone: 020 7947 7369
Fax: 020 7947 7656

The Court of Appeal Director's Office
Room E326
Telephone: 020 7947 6017
Fax: 020 7947 7495

The Area Director aims to resolve and respond to the complaint, giving you a full answer within 10 working days.

A leaflet called "I want to complain – what should I do" is available. For more information please ask one of the court staff or visit our website at:

www.hmcourts-service.gov.uk

We welcome suggestions and compliments too.

Whilst we can investigate complaints about how a judge, master or registrar behaved in court we cannot investigate anything to do with their judgment, their assessment of a case or overturn any of their decisions.

Information about how to make a complaint about the personal conduct of judges, masters or registrars is available on the web:

www.judicialcomplaints.gov.uk

Such complaints may be sent in writing to:

Office for Judicial Complaints (OJC),
4th Floor, Clive House,
70 Petty France,
London SW1H 9HD

Telephone: 020 7189 2937
Fax: 020 7189 2936

Your letter should include the name of the judge and court, your case number and the hearing date together with the specific details of the conduct about which you are complaining.

Although we cannot look into complaints about solicitors, barristers or any other organisation, you may find the following addresses useful:

Solicitors

Consumer Complaints Service,
The Law Society,
Victoria Court, 8 Dormer Place,
Leamington Spa,
Warwickshire CV32 5AE

Helpline: 0845 608 6565
Textphone: 0845 601 1682
Fax: 01926 431435
email: enquiries@lawsociety.org.uk
website: www.oss.lawsociety.org.uk

Barristers

If you would like a complaint form please write to:

The Complaints Department,
The General Council of the Bar,
Northumberland House,
289-293 High Holborn,
London WC1V 7HZ

Telephone: 020 7242 0082
Fax: 020 7611 1342
email: complaints@barcouncil.org.uk
website: www.barcouncil.org.uk

Straightforward Publishing

All titles, listed below, in the Straightforward Guides Series can be purchased online, using credit card or other forms of payment by going to www.straightfowardco.co.uk A discount of 25% per title is offered with online purchases.

Law
A Straightforward Guide to:
Consumer Rights
Bankruptcy Insolvency and the Law
Employment Law
Private Tenants Rights
Family law
Small Claims in the County Court
Contract law
Intellectual Property and the law
Divorce and the law
Leaseholders Rights
The Process of Conveyancing
Knowing Your Rights and Using the Courts
Producing Your own Will
Housing Rights
The Bailiff the law and You
Probate and The Law
Company law
What to Expect When You Go to Court
Guide to Competition Law
Give me Your Money-Guide to Effective Debt Collection
Caring for a Disabled Child

General titles
Letting Property for Profit

Buying, Selling and Renting property
Buying a Home in England and France
Bookkeeping and Accounts for Small Business

Creative Writing
Freelance Writing
Writing Your own Life Story
Writing performance Poetry
Writing Romantic Fiction
Speech Writing
Teaching Your Child to Read and write

Teaching Your Child to Swim
Raising a Child-The Early Years

Creating a Successful Commercial Website
The Straightforward Business Plan
The Straightforward C.V.
Successful Public Speaking

Handling Bereavement
Play the Game-A Compendium of Rules
Individual and Personal Finance
Understanding Mental Illness
The Two-Minute Message
Guide to Self Defence
Buying a Used Car
Tiling for Beginners

Go to:

www.straightforwardco.co.uk